RISJ ***CHALLENGES***

'Skyful of Lies' and Black Swans

The new tyranny of shifting information power in crises

Nik Gowing

REUTERS
INSTITUTE for the
STUDY of
JOURNALISM

Contents

Executive summary 1

1. Introduction 5

2. New media realities: the new vulnerability of power in a crisis 9

3. Challenge – what challenge? Is the media dynamic really so different? 17

4. New realities, old resistances: the 'one dime store in an E-Bay world' 19

5. First, fast, flawed and frightening: the tyranny of the time line 27

6. Fragmenting media space: the new asymmetric policy challenge from 'social media' 39

7. 'Bad apples' and 'failures in systems': the haunting pressure on credibility that never goes away 49

Abu Ghraib: the 'trophy' photos that haunted the Bush administration 50

Private Security Contractors: their activities exposed 52

Saddam Hussein's execution: the taunting that officials thought they had hidden 54

Iran: the real-time deceit that undermined its own propaganda push 56

Israel: lessons learned in 2006 but not mastered in 2009 57

Hurricane Katrina: how the media had better situational awareness than the US government 60

8. Burma and China 2008: contradictory approaches to new realities 63

Burma: street protests, a cyclone, and the 'Skyful of lies' 63

China: *weiji* – first a media crisis, then a media opportunity 66

The new common vulnerability for top–down information handling 74

9. The perspective: present and future? 77

Recommendations 78

Next stages for analysis 82

Acknowledgements 83

Executive summary

In a moment of major, unexpected crisis the institutions of power – whether political, governmental, military or corporate – face a new, acute vulnerability of both their influence and effectiveness. This study analyses the new fragility and brittleness of those institutions, and the profound impact upon them from a fast proliferating and almost ubiquitous breed of 'information doers'. Empowered by current, cheap lightweight, 'go anywhere' technologies available to all, they have an unprecedented mass ability to bear witness. The result is a matrix of real-time information flows that challenges the inadequacy of the structures of power to respond both with effective impact and in a timely way.

Exponential technological changes are redefining, broadening and fragmenting the media landscape in dramatic ways. They impact directly and profoundly by way of two new realities: first, on longstanding assumptions about the nature of the media in a crisis; secondly – and even more fundamentally – on the nature of power because the effectiveness of existing structures and their relations with the public are perceived as inadequate.

In a crisis there is a relentless and unforgiving trend towards an ever greater information transparency. In the most remote and hostile locations of the globe, hundreds of millions of electronic eyes and ears are creating a capacity for scrutiny and new demands for accountability. It is way beyond the assumed power and influence of the traditional media. This global electronic reach catches institutions unaware and surprises with what it reveals.

Overall, this surge of civilian information is having an asymmetric, negative impact on the traditional structures of power. It is subverting their effectiveness, and calling into question institutional assumptions that as organs of power they will function efficiently and with public confidence. With few exceptions, institutions of state, political and corporate power remain largely in denial about the inexorable negative impact on their reputations and the public's perceptions. Yet it is in times of acute crisis that expectations for effective action are greatest and most pressing.

These dramatic changes in the information dynamic have created what can be characterised as not just a Tyranny of Real Time but a Tyranny of the Time Line. At this critical information juncture, the time lines of media action and institutional reaction are increasingly out of sync. The moment any crisis incident takes place there is an imperative to fill the resulting information space within not hours but minutes, and if possible to dominate it. But the competition is ruthless and unforgiving. The new breed of 'information doers' enters that space immediately and relentlessly, first to bear witness digitally and then to transmit both the impressions and recorded material. And increasingly they do so overwhelmingly and more effectively.

Yet few institutions of government and corporate power, and those who work within them, readily understand and embrace this new reality, along with its profound implication for policy-making structures and effectiveness. Indeed, most actively resist them and remain way behind the curve. Too frequently they are unwilling to even contemplate or plan for the possibility of improbable Black Swan events that will undermine their perceived power and effectiveness. At the most extreme they even dismiss as a 'Skyful of Lies' the prolific real-time output from the new generation of information doers and 'social media' recording the unfolding events in a crisis.

The immediate policy challenge is to enter the information space with self-confidence and assertiveness as the media do, however incomplete the official understanding of the enormity of what is unfolding. Yet far too often the institutional systems and mindsets are neither prepared nor in place to match the flow of eye witness accounts and video that now proliferates almost instantly from the 'information doers'. This relative passivity is compounded by the latent but inappropriate fear of entering the space due to the inherent risks of being wrong or too hasty about the nature of the crisis.

This dilemma is defined as F3. It is the core challenge for both traditional media organisations and policy-makers alike in the minutes after a major crisis hits. The F3 options are neither easy nor comfortable. Should they be *first* to enter the information space? How *fast* should they do it? But how *flawed* might their remarks and first positions turn out to be in ways that could eventually undermine both public perceptions and confidence, and thereby rebound on institutional credibility?

Using a variety of examples, this paper analyses how when faced by the F3 challenge the institutional reaction is typically to hesitate and lose the initiative. This is because the mindsets relating to the nature of institutional power during a crisis remain largely intact and unreconstructed, despite the unrelenting changes in the real-time media environment. This study also provides examples of a small number of enlightened policy responses – but these are too few to suggest any sign of a fundamental shift in understanding and attitudes.

Overall this typical inaction, indifference and resistance to the new reality exacts a harsh price that undermines policy effectiveness and public confidence. To continue dismissing the real-time media pressures as marginal will further weaken the capacity of those institutions of power to convince the public and stakeholders that they are acting as appropriately and efficiently as the crisis requires.

The conclusion contains robust recommendations for how various institutions of political and corporate power must confront, understand and embrace the challenge of the new real-time 'information doer' and the implications. Most centre on the core weaknesses in both leadership skills and policy implementation systems.

In summary, the new real-time media realities are harsh. But once understood, embraced and acted upon the proposed solutions are compelling. They represent a path to institutional effectiveness and credibility when these are currently lacking.

1. Introduction

This study is the latest iteration in a process of analysis that I began in the mid-1990s when I was Diplomatic Editor at *Channel Four News*. A five-month sabbatical in the first half of 1994 at the Joan Shorenstein Center in the John F. Kennedy School at Harvard University allowed me to formulate an assessment of the state of the fast-emerging real-time media dynamic at that time. In what was still a nascent digital world I identified the challenge for the structures of both media and public policy as the 'tyranny of real time'. The resulting study,[1] and others that followed,[2] meant I set down a base-line framework for what inevitably has been a constant process of monitoring and assessment ever since. This discussion paper is a new audit of the current state of this relationship.

My subsequent work as a main presenter for the global channel BBC World News since 1996 has given me an unrivalled inside understanding of the changing dynamics at work on a 24/7 rolling news TV channel. I have been in the presenter's chair or in the newsroom experiencing at first hand the unfolding tensions and time lines during many crises.

The real-time role of a presenter in such moments of crisis, along with its responsibilities, is immortalised ten minutes into the movie *The Queen*. It centres on the drama surrounding the death of Princess Diana in August

[1] Nik Gowing, *Real-Time Television Coverage of Armed Conflicts and Diplomatic Crises: Does it Pressure or Distort Foreign Policy Decisions*? (Cambridge, MA: Joan Shorenstein Barone Center, John F. Kennedy School of Government, Harvard University, 1994).

[2] Nik Gowing, *Media Coverage: Help or Hindrance in Conflict Prevention* (Washington, DC: Carnegie Commission on Preventing Deadly Conflict, 1997). *New Challenges and Problems for Information Management in Complex Emergencies: Ominous Lessons Learned from the Great Lakes and Eastern Zaire in Late 1996 and early 1997* (London: ECHO in association with Save the Children Fund for the 'Dispatches From Disaster Conference', 28 May 1998). 'Information in Conflict: Who Really Commands the High Ground?' Annual lecture to the Liddell Hart Centre for Military Archives 2 March 2000. 'Real Time Crises: New Real Time Tensions', Paper prepared for the Royal United Services Institute and delivered at the RUSI/USJFCOM 'Military Operations on the Cusp' conference in Norfolk, Va., on 14–15 March 2005. Various updated iterations delivered at further security conferences, including a RUSI/USJFCOM follow up at the National Defense University, Washington, DC, on 17 Nov. 2005.

1997. Tony Blair is seen being woken by a call from the British ambassador in Paris to be given first news of the car crash in Paris. He then switches on the television to find out what is happening. I am the BBC presenter on air who provides him and a fast growing global audience with the latest, but incomplete news as it emerges. The film cuts to the sitting room of the Royal Family's summer residence at Balmoral in Scotland. The Queen, Queen Mother and Prince Philip are similarly shown relying on the rolling BBC news output for their first, primary information of the unfolding drama from Paris.

The trends in the relationship between a dramatically changing media environment and policy-making have been relentless and in many ways predictable. For a host of reasons they are uplifting and exciting for media practitioners, whether professionals or members of the new *ad hoc* breed of information doers that I identify in this study. Their capacity to record, reveal and report from anywhere has never been so unencumbered by technological limitations.

However, while positive for the broadening digital media landscape, the findings will make dark reading for those at the sharp end of political and corporate policy-making, especially in the field of security. The study is aimed primarily at them.

There is a new vulnerability for the institutions of public and corporate power, but many appear to be blind to the new dynamic. By and large there has been – and remains – institutional denial about its inexorable impact. The most obvious developments continue to be the most elusive when it comes to understanding the way assumed power and effectiveness are undermined by the new media transparency in a moment of acute crisis.

The experiences revealed by extensive interviewing, two brainstormings in Oxford hosted by the Reuters Institute, and detailed analysis of information handling in specific crises, seem to show that remarkably most in public service and corporate structures simply do not get it. Traditional mindsets and reactions continue to prevail while media realities shift at high speed in fresh and unforgiving directions.

As a result there is a new vulnerability, fragility and brittleness of power which weakens both the credibility and accountability of governments, the security organs and corporate institutions. This is often at the precise moment, during a time of adversity, that public opinion expects the optimum official assessments and leadership. This relentless trend will not be reversed, although there is a good chance that a new institutional willingness to open eyes to the new dynamic will mitigate its impact. But to achieve that there must be more official willingness to accept the scale and nature of the new media challenge detailed in this paper.

This analysis is the latest stage of work in progress. To tie down the trends has been like shooting at a constantly moving target that dives and soars, at times almost defying all efforts to capture the essence. This is the most up-to-date snapshot of a never-ending process. Therefore the text and conclusions cannot be definitive. They offer new vantage points and springboards for further analysis, discussion and insight. Multiple examples have been used to illustrate both the stark, emerging new principles and core dynamic. Together they highlight the vivid trend that signals why those in the field of policy-making must fully understand and appreciate the process now challenging the credibility and effectiveness of all they do on the public's behalf during these many times of crisis.

Setting out the challenge will prompt the inevitable question from policy-makers and those who serve them at all levels: 'So what do we do?' There is a summary of the main policy and practical options in the final section. But the core answer to that fundamental question is explicit in the many of the details of this analysis. Above all: do not deny but understand the inexorable dynamic at work that is both affecting and challenging all you do in the name of either your public constituency or your shareholders. This study highlights the high costs of not doing so.

In summary, the new real-time media realities are harsh. But once understood the nature of the solutions is a 'no brainer'.

2. New media realities: the new vulnerability of power in a crisis

In a moment of acute crisis, political and corporate leaders along with government officials are discovering they have far less power to shape public perceptions than they assume they must surely have *ex officio*.

There is a new democratisation of policy-making in crises which one former senior minister described as almost 'subversive'. One very senior official confirmed: 'We are in trouble! Those working in government are very much living in a different age.'[3] Another said: 'officials are living on a different planet if they think they control all the levers of policy now and in the future' during a major crisis.

This study confirms that their power is more fragile and vulnerable than most realise or care to admit. By and large there remains a self-deluding mindset of denial. Black Swan incidents[4] which could one day threaten both institutional effectiveness and reputations tend to be viewed as either inconceivable or too improbable to have to prepare for, especially the new media implications.

Yet when such crises unfold, the level of public respect for the systems of institutional power is more brittle than assumed. This is because these systems

[3] This experience confirms more structured analysis and observations in works like David S. Alberts and Richard E. Hayes, *Power to the Edge: Command . . . Control . . . in the Information Age* (Washington, DC: DoD Command and Control Research Program, 2004).They write, e.g. (p. 175): 'The problems military organisations face and the nature of the tasks undertaken have grown in complexity and require ever more rapid responses. Constraints on information flows prevent the timely development of situation awareness while constraints on command approach and asset utilisation make it more difficult to respond appropriately and/or rapidly.' They conclude (p. 234): 'Given the significant advances in technology, the primary barriers that remain are cultural and institutional. Finding ways to remove these impediments to progress is on the critical path to transformation. Education alone will not be sufficient.'

[5] Adapted from the Black Swan principle identified by Nassim Nicholas Taleb in his book *The Black Swan: The Impact of the Highly Improbable* (London: Allen Lane, 2007). Taleb writes that 'We don't learn that we don't learn'; that there is a 'severe limitation to our learning from observations or experience, and the fragility of our knowledge'; he identifies 'our blindness with respect to randomness, particularly the large deviations'.

and the processes of democratic governance face harsh challenges from new technologies and information dynamics. Together they are driving this wave of democratisation and empowerment that shifts and redefines the nature of power in a crisis.

Overall there is a new capacity for scrutiny and accountability way beyond the assumed power and influence of the traditional media. The reasons are twofold. First, technical change has dramatically foreshortened the news and information cycle from a few hours to often no more than a few minutes. Second, there is now a proliferation of hundreds of millions of 'information doers' who have dramatically modified and broadened the assumed definitions of the media in a crisis. They shed light where it is often assumed officially there will be darkness.

Each of these two reasons has provided fundamental new challenges. But when acting together their impact can be devastating. The long-held conventional wisdom of a gulf in time and quality between the *news* that signals an event and the *truth* eventually emerging[5] is fast being eliminated. Instead of multiplying the 'tendency to recycle ignorance' and 'information chaos' through 'churnalism', as suggested by Nick Davies,[6] there is typically a dramatic and timely promotion of both knowledge and insight. This dynamic is sharpened because the time lines of media and of power are increasingly out of sync. As a result, the new reality repeatedly challenges, then threatens, political and institutional power. It also distorts the credibility of leaderships and those who serve them.

In a crisis, the public now often know much of what is taking place before those in power have a first grip on developments, let alone time to pre-empt and mediate the message in an authoritative way. The information transparency created by mobile phones and all forms of digital connectivity immediately challenges the assumptions of political, military and corporate leaderships that the public trust whatever actions are undertaken in their name.[7] It also swiftly generates a public expectation of official omnipotence and perfect knowledge. Both are simply unrealistic in the multi-platform, 24/7 real-time information environment.

Hence the growing vulnerability, fragility and brittleness of power in a sudden crisis. One British cabinet minister has gone as far as to label this

[5] First identified by Walter Lippmann in *Public Opinion* (1922). In ch. 24 Lippmann wrote: that while the 'function of news is to signalize an event, the function of truth is to bring to light the hidden facts, to set them into relation with each other, and make a picture of reality on which men can act'. Lippmann contended that a journalist's view is through 'subjective lenses', so news is 'imperfectly recorded' and its role as 'an organ of direct democracy' is questionable. Book reprinted by Free Press, 1997. Also available at http://xroads.virginia.edu/~Hyper2/CDFinal/Lippman/cover.html from the University of Virginia.

[6] A central theme in Nick Davies, *Flat Earth News: An Award-winning Reporter Exposes Falsehood, Distortion and Propaganda in the Global Media* (London: Vintage Books, 2008).

[7] For wider analysis of this growing risk in the political assumption of public trust see e.g. Chris Patten, *Not Quite the Diplomat* (London: Penguin, 2006), 114.

shifting of power from the state to citizens as the new 'civilian surge'.[8] It is energised by dramatic innovations in digital technology. They have created a media spectrum and matrix that has rapidly become far wider, deeper, more multi-dimensional and all-pervasive than the traditional, conventional (and often disparaging) assumptions concerning the 'reptiles' of 'the damn *meejah*'[9] made by those in the highest positions of responsibility and influence.

The reasons and explanations for this are straightforward. The digital trend has been identified,[10] yet voices of enlightenment still tend to be the exception.[11] The most obvious remains frequently the most elusive. While many of the individual dots in the matrix are understood, they are rarely joined up so that the sweeping implications for crisis policy-making are fully appreciated. As a result they remain little understood, especially by many of the most powerful figures in the political and corporate world who still use 'stereotypes as a defence'.[12] There are occasional radical beacons of insight[13] where insiders believe there is a system with a 'shit hot' ability to counter the real-time impact of digital camera imagery in a sudden crisis. But it remains remarkable, and a matter of concern, how many top–down government and corporate power structures still largely fail to embrace the stark, but exciting realities of instant digital communications. This is even though they are now known to most people and available worldwide to almost anyone who can afford them.

Yet these new Black Swan realities routinely blind-side them. Exposed, they are forced into often inappropriate tactical reactions at the expense of strategic policy-making. In this digital age the adage from the Middle Ages that 'in the land of the blind, the one-eyed man is king'[14] has fresh relevance. But the

[8] Remarks made by British Foreign Secretary David Miliband to British ambassadors at the Foreign Office's Heads of Mission conference in the QE2 Centre, London, on 4 March 2008.

[9] Descriptions coined by British UNPROFOR military spokesman during the Balkan wars of the 1990s.

[10] See e.g. the work of Professor Helen Margetts at the Oxford Internet Institute.

[11] See Jeremy Greenstock, 'States Must Act Locally in a Globalised World', *Financial Times* (15 May 2008): 'Slowly, the structures and instruments of the state are losing their power to produce what we demand of them. Few policies can cope with the complexity of it all. Too often, the reactive replaces the strategic. Globalisation and the spread of freedom are not only redistributing to new players, across borders, the access to economic growth and political influence, they are changing the relationship between citizen and state, within societies. . . . The gap is growing between macro-level policymaking and effective implementation. Government, not just in the UK, is losing its reputation for competence; the citizen is becoming less respectful of authority.'

[12] Lippmann, *Public Opinion*, ch. 7.

[13] After years lagging behind the curve, sources confirm that during 2007–8 the British Foreign Office radically enhanced its capacity to match the new real-time media capabilities. An FCO paper also confirmed two options when faced with the new realities: 'One is to run and hide, the other is to engage. Our vision is of engagement.' Jim Murphy (ed.), *Engagement: Public Diplomacy in a Globalised World* (London: Foreign and Commonwealth Office, July 2008), foreword. Access via www.fco.gov.uk/en/about-the-fco/publications/publications/pd-publication/ (Murphy MP is a former Minister for Europe, whose responsibilities included policy on Public Diplomacy).

[14] Desiderius Erasmus, *Adagia*, *c.*1508.

institutional instinct tends to be one of resistance.[15] The standard and quality of leadership is one of the outstanding weaknesses identified in the fine-tuning of British strategy to ensure national resilience during an overwhelming crisis. Bruce Mann, director of the UK Civil Contingencies Secretariat, revealed that 'I know after four years [in the post] what bad crisis leadership is. But defining what is good in this soft environment is really quite complex.'[16] Instead of adapting nimbly, the systemic mindsets of governmental and corporate structures tend to have feet of clay.[17] Insiders at the highest levels confirm this is because the mind-walls[18] relating to the nature of institutional power during a crisis remain largely intact and unreconstructed. Until very recently, most even dismissed these pressures as marginal. To continue doing so will further weaken their capacity to handle a crisis.

As one former senior minister confirmed: 'The whole culture has to change.' Most in high positions of power and responsibility fail to identify a Black Swan reality until it first wrongfoots, then overtakes them. Some have conceded that the abrupt realisation of a new vulnerability in their executive power is a shock. By that time any chance of retaining the policy initiative is long past, the public perception of competence and effectiveness is often weakened, and the high ground lost. It is then frequently too late to retake it.

In other words, the systems of governance and policy oversight are both flawed and inadequate. In government cabinet rooms, ministerial offices, military and security command HQs, or many corporate board rooms there is little fundamental systemic change either to embrace or to match the hyper rates of technological media developments.[19] This is even though most of those involved readily use privately the cheap, lightweight technology that now challenges their professional duties.

So what is the fundamental change that causes such difficulties? There is a new media which stretches the definition far beyond the traditional understanding and assumptions of what 'media' involves. Most profound is the transparency and mass power to bear witness created by the ubiquity

[15] For an insight into the instinctive executive and institutional caution towards embracing new realities see e.g. Charles Leadbeater, *We Think: The Power of Mass Creativity* (London: Profile Books, 2008). The first line of the book is 'If you are not perplexed, you should be'.

[16] Remarks to a RUSI conference in London on 8 Oct. 2008. 'UK Resilience 2008: Contributions to Resilience'.

[17] For one confirmation of the frequent inability to embrace lessons acquired across multiple crises see: Patrick Cockburn, 'A Fatal Detachment from Reality: How Bush's Failures in Iraq and New Orleans are Linked', *Independent* (10 Sept. 2005).

[18] 'Mind-wall' is a liberal reinterpretation of a concept identified by Timothy Garton Ash relating to the 'walls of ignorance, selfishness and prejudice' in his book *Free World: America, Europe and the Surprising Future of the West* (New York: Random House, 2004). See the opening section 'To the Reader'.

[19] In 'Lack of Planning: America's Real Disaster', *Independent on Sunday* (11 Sept. 2005), Bruce Nussbaum of *Business Week* describes 'deeply flawed organisations beset by poor management, siloed cultures and inadequate communication' which are ill-prepared for handling the 'worst case' extreme pressures of a crisis on their personnel and structures.

of new, cheap digital technology. The explosive growth of its use by almost anybody with the modest amount of cash needed to lease or buy devices is now well developed and taken for granted. But joining up the dots to define the implications for power and policy-makers is far less developed and appreciated. So too is any forensic understanding of the often breath-taking change underway, as even the most senior media insiders concede.[20]

This proliferation of tiny cameras, mobile phones, PDAs and ever more available bandwidth is not just in the urban sprawls of developed countries. It should now be taken for granted in the most obscure, unlikely and remote locations of the globe. That means the most distant can instantly become the most immediate, and therefore the most challenging for policy-makers in a moment of crisis.

The tens of millions of new electronic eyes and ears spawned by these pocket technologies are now in the hands of a new mass breed of 'information doers'. Not only do they bear witness. They have the capacity to record what they see, then transmit in real time both the images and their impressions by way of blogs or emails. While there is no distinction by age, income or social strata, that ability and propensity to become an 'information doer' tends to be greatest among the younger generation. They are the fast-emerging cohort, and the embedded digital information realities are almost in their DNA. Hence their new classification as the 'Born Digitals',[21] although there are disputed views on the precise nature of this next generation dynamic and whether such a catchy description is yet justified.

Using the cheap, ever more powerful digital technology carried in their pockets, cargo pants, shoulder bags or military webbing, they provide at high speed a proliferation of crude, almost instant views of unfolding events on a growing multitude of unmediated media platforms. The rapid proliferation of 3G connectivity and Wi Fi, often in those remote and unlikely locations,[22] has dramatically enhanced this impact. The imminent roll out of Wi-Max[23] and 4G will be another significant leap forward in connectivity and reducing costs, which will further exacerbate pressure on policy-making. *Time* magazine named its person of the year at the end of 2006 as 'You' because 'You control

[20] For a snapshot of the latest uncertainties about the future nature and business models of media see the Director's report from the Ditchley Foundation's conference on 'The Media and Democracy', 4–6 Dec. 2008; available at www.ditchley.co.uk/page/337/media-and-democracy.htm

[21] See e.g. John Palfrey and Urs Gasser, *Born Digitals: Understanding the First Generation of Digital Natives* (New York: Basic Books, 2008). This is a sociological study that details the first generation of 'Digital Natives' – children who were born into and raised in the digital world. They are coming of age. It analyses how the world will be reshaped in their image. Also the regular webletter *Born Digital Daily: Making the Internet a Better Place Since Birth* posted by www.undercurrent.com

[22] Bruce Hoffman, 'Cellphones in the Hindu Kush', *The National Interest* (July–Aug. 2008).

[23] Wi-Max will facilitate the live plugging in almost anywhere of cameras loaded with a Wi Fi card. This will mean high quality, vivid imagery in real time. Costs will be reduced. Access will be increased. *See Financial Times Business Supplement* (18 June 2008), 1.

the Information Age'. So 'Welcome to your world' it added. *Time* reinforced the impact of its message with a twenty-first-century version of the big index finger pointing forward derived from the British First World War recruiting poster that declared 'Your country needs you'.[24]

No one sets out each day aiming to be a pivotal doer of information that might rock a government or corporation in a crisis. After all, the nature of most crises is that they are both unexpected and profound in their consequences. But a pivotal role in cutting edge information flows is what can happen to those information doers who find themselves in the heart of dramatic, unfolding events. They are the primary recorders of what happens before their eyes and camera lens, whether in a massive natural disaster like the Asia tsunami of 2004 or the many extremes of violent armed conflict. They can be eye witnesses or protesters nipping into an internet cafe in Rangoon, monks in Lhasa transmitting snatched mobile phone images, hurricane victims with a cell phone in the New Orleans Superdome, or casual recorders of unfolding, inappropriate police behaviour as in London during the anti-G20 demonstrations of 1 April 2009.[25] Their influence will be via the mainstream traditional media outlets. It will also be well beyond, via the vast and growing proliferation of usually unmediated content platforms of the new 'social media'.

In bearing witness, these hundreds of millions of new players in the information space have a capacity to generate content and 'neighbour' information[26] on an almost infinite number of media platforms. For all of them, price and technological complexity are no longer a barrier to accessing the new media matrix. Nor is lack of bravado or a willingness to take risks.[27] They often include some of the poorest or least likely wielders of video equipment in any community. They also include workers in aid agencies or

[24] Cover story, *Time* (25 Dec. 2006/1 Jan. 2007).

[25] See Paul Lewis, 'Revealed: Video of Police Attack on Man Who Died at G20 Protest', *Guardian* (8 Apr. 2009). A chance video taken by a New York investment banker showed the moment newspaper seller Ian Tomlinson was hit by a policeman's baton and fell to the ground shortly before he died. This 'information doer' video – along with more which emerged of other incidents in London – showed apparent police use of disproportionate force. In subsequent days the videos and other evidence challenged the police justification of tactics and the credibility of its version of incidents. They forced a series of independent investigations of police behaviour and tactics, and put them on the political agenda. The original video prompted a second post-mortem which discovered that Mr Tomlinson did not die of a heart attack as first reported by police, but 'internal bleeding'.

[26] Holly Yeager, 'Are you being Listserved?', *Financial Times* (12/13 May 2007).

[27] A vast range of examples confirms this reality. See e.g. the images grabbed by passengers running for their lives after an Air France plane skidded off the runway and threatened to explode at Toronto airport in a storm on 2 Aug. 2005. Or the video taken by residents defying fears of massive contamination after an enormous explosion at the Buncefield jet aviation fuel terminal north of London on 11 Dec. 2005. Or the video from passengers on QANTAS flight QF30 who recorded the sudden decompression of their Boeing 747-400 after an onboard explosion ripped out part of the fuselage after leaving Hong Kong on 25 July 2008.

NGOs determined to get greater public awareness of their mission,[28] a vast array of campaigners and advocates for a cause,[29] or those like insurgent sympathisers[30] and terrorists who want to highlight in real time the impact of their violent actions using what could be labelled ITV – Insurgent Television.[31] Often they are more media-savvy and smarter at information operations than the conventional forces they are fighting – like the Americans or British.[32] Like any good news organisation the Taleban, for example, makes sure their website is updated at least hourly.[33]

All these activists, and the new wielders of digital recording or uploading capacity, are now members of the media, with the potential to have the same prominence and impact as the brand names of traditional media outlets.[34] This

[28] See Glenda Cooper, 'Anyone Here Survived a Wave, Speak English and Got a Mobile? The Media, Aid Agencies and Reporting Disasters since the Tsunami', paper delivered on 5 Nov. 2007. Available at: http://64.233.183.104/search?q=cache:gXIleRuyprsJ:www.nuffield.ox.ac.uk/Guardian/Nuffield%2520Guardian%2520Lecture%25202007.pdf+Anyone+here+survived+a+wave,+speak+English+and+got+a+mobile&hl=en&ct=clnk&cd=3&gl=uk

[29] See e.g. the advocacy work of B'tselem, the Israeli campaigning organisation for human rights. In 2007 B'tselem issued 100 video cameras to willing but untrained members of their cause in the Palestinian territories. This made each of those video activists new members of the media. B'tselem labelled the initiative as 'Shooting Back'. It was designed to create a network of activists who would record on video the allegedly unlawful activities of the Israeli Defence Forces. In this way B'tselem believed they would generate material for the traditional media platforms. It would also create a public profile for what is taking place and mean IDF soldiers will be held to public account for violating both international laws and principles. See e.g. www.btselem.org/english/Firearms/20080721_Nilin_Shooting.asp

[30] For details of Al-Zawraa TV broadcast from an unknown location in the Middle East see Michael Howard, 'Insurgent TV Channel Turns into Iraq's Newest Cult Hit', *Guardian* (15 Jan. 2008).

[31] One of many examples: the insurgents who shot down a British Special Forces C-130 transport plane over Iraq between Baghdad and Balad on 31 Jan. 2005 were accompanied by a video camera. It recorded both what appeared to be the rocket being fired then the immediate aftermath of the wreckage on the ground. Just like orthodox coverage by traditional media organisations, the insurgents 'filed' their video material quickly. It rapidly became available to news agencies. Once validated with British military confirmation that they had lost the aircraft, the material became the prime source for standard news coverage throughout the subsequent news cycle. The option of using the insurgent material as a core part of news coverage raises complex ethical issues. But such material now has to be considered an uneasy part of the new media mix. The same can be said of video material shot by terrorists like those who seized the school in Beslan in Sept. 2004. They had planned to use their graphic video coverage of the hundreds of teenagers held hostage as part of their own media information campaign. While uncomfortable for traditional media outlets to make use of, their video material provided an emotional insight into the nature of the hostage operation they planned.

[32] Hoffman, 'Cellphones in the Hindu Kush'.

[33] 'When I started I had six fighters. Now I have 500.' Special report on the Taleban by Ghaith Abdul-Ahad. *Guardian* (15 Dec. 2008), 5.

[34] The rapid blurring of lines between traditional and new media is well illustrated by Kevin Sites. He had worked for TV news outlets, reporting and producing news in the well-established ways of the US networks. Then he set himself up as the 'first internet correspondent for Yahoo! News'. At the time Yahoo was a strong brand on the internet but an upstart unknown in the business and skills of news. Sites travelled to 'virtually every major hot spot'. 'Armed with just a video camera, a digital camera, a laptop and a satellite modem' he was able to produce some remarkable insights into the most unpleasant sides of conflict. He is best known for recording a US Marine shooting dead an injured Iraqi insurgent holed up in a mosque in Fallujah in Nov. 2004. At the time he was a freelance embedded with NBC News. See Kevin Sites, *In the Hot Zone: One Man, One Year, Twenty Wars* (New York: Harper Perennial, 2007).

includes those with the most evil of intentions.[35] In the security environment this has created what British Defence Secretary John Reid confirmed is an 'uneven battlefield of one-sided scrutiny', which is facilitating a new 'asymmetric – uneven – scrutiny of warfare'.[36] Encouragingly, those words were remarkably similar to my own analysis in a paper delivered to security conferences one year earlier.[37]

But to describe these 'information doers' or 'motivated amateurs' as 'citizen journalists' is a step too far. More appropriate is the emerging lexicon related to 'social media' which does not imply the use of traditional mediated processes of journalism. The best high-value brands in the traditional media will always want to check facts and mediate scrupulously the material these new 'information doers' provide in order to protect their brand reputation. After all, the intent and technological capacity to manipulate or deceive from anywhere in this digital world is well proven.[38] Any insiders who violate these principles face summary dismissal.[39] In the end any semantic differences over the phrase or label to describe them should come second to accepting that they are increasingly significant, contributing, *ad hoc* members of a media matrix which is now broader, deeper and more multi-layered.

Simultaneously, other media demarcation lines are becoming blurred too. For example, in late 2008 the mass-circulation German newspaper *Bild* joined up with supermarket chain Lidl to sell a simple-to-use digital camera for €70 to help develop its 'volksjournalismus' (people's journalism) project. The result will be a 'staff increase of 82 million'! One media expert believed such new consumer empowerment could even 'lead to the improvement of standards as readers demand a higher quality'.[40] Another example is the non-professional photo-sharing site Flickr which has gone into partnership with the professional agency Getty Images. The Big Pictures agency has spawned Mr Paparazzi which pushes the possibility of anyone to make money from images under the catch line: 'Now EVERYONE's a paparazzo!'

[35] President Bush used his radio address on 21 Feb. 2006 to deliver this description: 'They have a sophisticated propaganda strategy. They know they cannot defeat us in the battle, so they conduct high-profile attacks, hoping that the images of violence will demoralize our country and force us to retreat. They carry video cameras and film their atrocities, and broadcast them on the Internet. They e-mail images and video clips to Middle Eastern cable networks like al-Jazeera, and instruct their followers to send the same material to American journalists, authors, and opinion leaders. They operate websites, where they post messages for their followers and readers across the world.'

[36] Speech to Kings College, London, 20 Feb. 2006.

[37] Gowing, 'Real Time Crises' (2005).

[38] There is a host of examples, whether sinister from war zones or light hearted for fun. One of the best was a photo labelled 'Exclusive: First-Ever Pictures of the World's ONLY Flying Penguins', *Daily Mirror* (1 Apr. 2008). The date should have immediately created suspicions. But the brilliantly doctored photo and accompanying paragraphs fooled many into believing a BBC crew had really discovered flying penguins which were 'the perfect example of Darwin's theory of evolution working in reverse'.

[39] Raymond Snoddy, 'Reuters: How to Save the Face of a Venerable News Organisation', *Independent* (12 Feb. 2007), details how Reuters acted quickly after bloggers noticed that two photographs of smoke rising after Israeli air strikes in Beirut during the 2006 war had been 'materially altered'.

[40] Kate Connolly, 'Bild Announces Staff Increase of 82 Million', *Guardian* (8 Dec. 2008).

3. Challenge – what challenge? Is the media dynamic really so different?

Historians and others writing on policy have long identified critical pressures on ministers and officials from the public perceptions created by media coverage in times of war or crisis. Lord Hankey, in his lectures reviewing *Government Control in War,*[41] wrote in 1945 of the impact on the 'human factor' of the 'increasing tempo of government business' resulting from 'modern developments' that had 'brought great changes' in relations between ministers and officials. Hugh Wilson[42] quotes the former Foreign Secretary, Sir Edward Grey,[43] who wrote in his memoirs that 'during his term of office he was so pressed that he could not remember having taken any step that was not of immediate urgency and for the solving of a problem directly in front of him'.

After his many years in different high-level positions of national and multi-national public responsibility, Chris Patten wrote: 'a new calamity can always knock you off course; another day's headline can impose short-term decisions that threaten long term-objectives'.[44] This kneejerk rush to short-term decisions can leave 'bureaucratic confusion and policy discontinuity in their wake'. The chair of the US Senate Foreign Relations Committee during the Vietnam war, Senator J. William Fulbright, highlighted in his book, *The Arrogance of Power,* the vulnerability of policy-makers and 'powerful nations' to world opinion and perceptions. 'Much more than in the past' the US would have to 'make a good case for our policies before the bar of world opinion'.[45] In his analysis of 'ethnic war and the modern conscience' during the 1990s

[41] Lord Hankey, *Government Control in War* (London: Cambridge University Press, 1945), 76.

[42] Hugh Wilson, *Education of a Diplomat* (London: Longmans, Green & Co. 1938), 47.

[43] Sir Edward Grey served two terms as British Foreign Secretary, 1892–5 and 1905–16.

[44] Patten, *Not Quite the Diplomat,* 164.

[45] J. William Fulbright, *The Arrogance of Power* (London: Pelican, 1970). See the preface by Francis O. Wilcox, p. 9.

Michael Ignatieff described how television has become 'the instrument of a new kind of politics'.[46] It has created a new imperative for accountability and 'managed to force governments to pay some degree of attention to the public relations costs of their exercises in domestic repression', so bringing 'political intentions and their consequences face to face with each other'. Peter Feaver has highlighted the risks and costs to government systems, especially the military, in failing to appreciate the newly evolving relationship created by public awareness of policy being enacted in their name.[47]

Kishore Mahbubani, Singapore's former UN ambassador who is now dean of the Lee Kuan Yew School of Public Policy, highlights how 'daily, billions of eyes are watching, studying and judging' a nation like the United States. This is by way of digital connectivity, and most critically it creates instant, usually unfavourable perceptions.[48]

So in many ways this core dynamic and the forces at work are not new. But the relentless nutcracker pressures of time and real-time transparency are. So are the fragmentation and low-tech empowerment of the media space.

This is the tyrannical impact of shifting information power in a crisis.

[46] Michael Ignatieff, *The Warrior's Honor* (London: Chatto & Windus, 1998), 21–2.

[47] Peter D. Feaver, *Armed Servants: Agency, Oversight, and Civil–Military Relations* (Cambridge, Mass.: Harvard University Press, 2003).

[48] Kishore Mahbubani, *Beyond the Age of Innocence* (New York: Public Affairs, 2005), p. xix.

4. New realities, old resistances: the 'one dime store in an E-Bay world'

The trend of the new transparency is that it catches unaware and surprises with what it reveals. Many at the highest official levels confess frankly they find this new reality inconvenient. So traditional instincts and systems live on, with the continuing – but misplaced – assumptions of information superiority and ultimately dominance.[49] As a result, new working practices are rarely put in place to cope, and the implications of media developments tend not to be audited in the fundamental ways needed[50]. Instead, the primary imperative tends to be protecting the status quo at all costs.[51] The main instinct continues to be the belief that some variant of spin will comfortably ensure official dominance of the information High Ground. In some cases this can be reinforced by a communications strategy that employs official bullying and – if necessary – dishonesty to ensure continued information supremacy.[52]

Even occasional official political alerts about the inevitability of an ever sharper challenge from the new media realities seem to find little resonance

[49] To sample the institutional military stresses of coming to terms with the new information realities see Thomas X Hammes, *The Sling and the Stone* (St Paul, Minn.: Zenith Press, 2004). Hammes observes *inter alia*: 'Just as the world has evolved from an industrial society to an information-based society, so has warfare. Information collection against today's threats requires a greater investment in human skills. Technology by itself is not the answer. The US Defense establishment's failure to address the importance of human knowledge over that of technology leaves us unprepared to deal with the kind of wars we are fighting today, and those we are most likely to face in the future – fourth generation wars.'

[50] Joseph S. Nye, *The Power to Lead* (New York: Oxford University Press, 2008), 1 and 105-9 ('Information Flows') confirm the developing evidence of the new core leadership challenge for 'politics and organisations'.

[51] See Lawrence Freedman, *Transformation in Strategic Affairs* (London: Routledge, 2006). This Adelphi Paper for the IISS details the problems US Forces have had adapting from regular wars to irregular conflicts where conflict is part of, and embedded in, the structures of society.

[52] To sample this kind of mindset see Adam Boulton, *Tony's Ten Years: Memories of the Blair Administration* (London: Simon & Schuster, 2008).

in calls for systemic change.[53] US Defence Secretary Donald Rumsfeld once lambasted the institutions of government for being 'like a one dime store in an E-Bay World' because of their slowness to react.[54] But a host of sources have confirmed that entrenched resistance to embracing the new transparent realities of the ICT's 'E-Bay World' remains. At their most extreme the responses can even be obstructive, evasive and even murderous.[55] Because of the potential impact of what they record, those using the new media technology – whether the professionals or the proliferating mass of public practitioners – have increasingly been targeted with lethal force by those determined to shut down anyone who is part of creating the new transparency. This is even though in a war zone they are unarmed, civilian non-combatants as defined in the Geneva conventions.

This shocking official intolerance by some in power of those information doers with the capacity to both record and reveal goes a long way to explaining why 'the price of truth has gone up grievously'.[56] That may sound dramatic. But outrageously sometimes those civilians with cameras or mobile phones are regarded as armed combatants, with their electronic eyes and ears categorised as a 'lethal weapon' that justifies a response using deadly force. This grave concern explains the remarkable success of media pressures at the UN Security Council which two days before Christmas in 2006 achieved UN Security Resolution 1738 to protect journalists and media operatives in conflict situations.[57] It confirmed first the widespread nature of the threat to them, then the imperative and right to ensure they work freely and safely. Yet deeply troubling official indifference to this new principle remains.

One of many examples was the Associated Press photographer, Bilal Hussein. He was held by US forces in Iraq for two years, allegedly for being 'a terrorist media operative' because of material and photos found in his house.

[53] A conference of leading diplomats and journalists in May 2005 on 'World Opinion and Public Diplomacy: How Should Policy Makers Influence and be Influenced?' drew two important conclusions: (1) 'As the world changes to become even more in formation-aware, government skills seem to be declining'; (2) 'Policy makers have to re-think the basis of their approach to Public Diplomacy if they are to achieve the right sort of impact on both their domestic and international audiences'. The meeting was convened in Cantigny, Ill., by the Chicago Council on Foreign Relations and Ditchley Foundation on 4–6 May 2005.

[54] US Defence Secretary Donald Rumsfeld told the US Council on Foreign Relations on 17 Feb. 2006: 'Our enemies have skilfully adapted to fight wars in today's media age, but for the most part we . . . our government has not adapted.' He described this as an 'unacceptable, dangerous deficiency'. He said government must 'develop an institutional capacity to anticipate and act within the same news cycle'. Whether by coincidence or political design, British Defence Secretary John Reid repeated the analysis to Kings College on 20 Feb. 2006. He concluded that as a result 'we all need to get smarter and understand this new battlespace better'.

[55] For the scale and nature of these attacks consult the work of NGOs campaigning for the rights of journalists and media workers in war zones, especially the International News Safety Institute (www.newssafety.com), the Rory Peck Trust (www.rorypecktrust.org), Reporters Without Borders (www.rsf.org).

[56] See the report on the new threats to media workers in *Killing the Messenger* (Brussels: International News Safety Institute, 2006).

[57] UNSCR passed on 23 Dec. 2006 resolved *inter alia* that 'journalists, media professionals and associated personnel engaged in dangerous professional missions in areas of armed conflicts shall be considered civilians, to be respected and protected as such'.

He was released without charge or explanation on 16 April 2008.

A second example: on 17 April 2008 Reuters cameraman Fadel Shana was killed in Gaza by multiple flechette darts from an Israeli tank shell which he videoed being fired from a nearby hill. Shana and his soundman were wearing blue flak jackets marked in large letters with the word PRESS. Their vehicle also had bold PRESS and TV markings. Yet the Israeli military's advocate general decided four months later that the tank crew's view that Shana and his camera were 'hostile' and 'carrying an object most likely to be a weapon' was a 'reasonable conclusion'.[58] Both Reuters and the Foreign Press Association in Tel Aviv expressed dismay and contempt for this apparent official complicity in 'deadly negligence'. Most troubling is that Fadel Shana's death was merely the latest of many incidents over several years where IDF soldiers had targeted camera operators and media workers with deadly force.

A third example occurred three months after the passing of the UN resolution. In March 2007 a US commander in Nangarhar, Afghanistan, thought it acceptable to 'rip cameras from local reporters' and 'delete their pictures' after a convoy of US marines shot at least 10 people and wounded 33 following a suicide attack. The US marines were part of a multinational deployment to create the conditions in Afghanistan for an open society and good governance. That should include first developing then preserving the rights of a free media. So how, then, could a US commander believe he would get away with justifying the action on the basis that 'untrained' Afghans might 'capture visual details that were not as they originally were'?[59] After a widespread public outcry, the marines involved were eventually returned to the US, and their officers charged. But once again, a military investigation process cleared them of responsibility for what were later confirmed as 16 deaths.[60]

In Iraq in 2007 the Indian cameraman Ashwin Raman was chronicling the anti-insurgent operations of one unit of US troops. While embedded with them to record unfolding events he encountered a reluctant tolerance of his palm-sized camera as it recorded the unit's darker incidents and sometimes unlawful behaviour. But the soldiers made clear to him that they would take decisive action against any unauthorised cameras they spotted. For editorial balance Raman then spent time on the other side of the front line with the Mahdi army to record their view of the US troops he had previously been with. The Mahdi army insisted that even his small camera made him too vulnerable, so they only allowed him to use the lens in his mobile phone. Raman's reflections on how the US troops would now view him and his

[58] The IDF advocate general's report was published on 13 Aug. 2008.

[59] The incident was on 4 Mar. 2007. Reporting is taken from Declan Walsh, 'US and Kabul Officials Get Tough with Journalists Amid Growing Insurgent Violence', *Guardian* (26 Apr. 2007).

[60] Clancy Chassay, 'I was Still Holding My Grandson's Hand: The Rest was Gone', *Guardian* (16 Dec. 2008).

tiny camera are salutary in their confirmation of the official mindset about the media 'threat'. He described his thoughts as he was covertly filming an Abrams tank from the Mahdi army's viewpoint. 'I had this small camera, this Nokia telephone camera. And they saw me. I thought they would shoot me, you know. But they did not. They just went by. It was a very, very, very scary moment!'[61]

Of equal concern are official efforts to marginalise the impact of material emerging in the new digitally transparent media environment. Typically there is no culture in the US forces especially of mounting a timely, pre-emptive investigation into any alleged targeting errors involving casualties. In late 2008, Human Rights Watch criticised this US mindset in Afghanistan as 'unilateral, ponderous, and lacking in transparency', thereby 'undercutting rather than improving relations with local populations and the Afghan government'.[62] The same culture had prevailed for longer in Iraq. After the 'information doer' video camera of a neighbour recorded the bloody aftermath of a highly questionable incident in which 24 Iraqis were killed by US Marines in Haditha on 19 November 2005, the official systems did all they could to protect their own. Despite the video evidence of a 'massacre' by US troops, eye witness accounts[63] and subsequent confirmation in a *Time* magazine investigation,[64] military charges against indicted marines[65] were progressively diluted from second degree murder to lesser charges, with most marines acquitted early on.

In Afghanistan most of the targeting errors by US-led warplanes that resulted in high civilian casualties have never been admitted to willingly by the military. Frequently those who have survived or witnessed an alleged case of mistaken targeting have been unable to produce compelling evidence to challenge credibly the US military's version. Even after NATO confirmed in early 2008 that targeting procedures were inadequate and must be tightened up, apparent errors continued. But on each occasion the reality of what took place had to be forced from the military belatedly and reluctantly. In several cases, only video shot by an information doer forced accountability where otherwise there would probably have been none.

One air strike on 22 August 2008 became emblematic of this deep tension of principles. US-led NATO troops on a ground operation in Azizabad near Herat in the west of the country had been pinned down by Taleban forces.

[61] Ashwin Raman was a finalist for the Rory Peck Features Award 2007. Quotes taken from *The Firing Line*, transmitted on BBC World News and BBC News during late Nov. 2007.

[62] *Troops in Contact: Airstrikes and Civilian Deaths in Afghanistan* (New York: Human Rights Watch, 7 Sept. 2008).

[63] 'The Marines and a "Massacre" in Iraq: US Troops to Face Homicide Charges Amid Horror Claims', *The Times* (27 May 2006).

[64] 'Inside Haditha: Inside the Investigation', *Time* (12 June 2006), cover story.

[65] See *Guardian* (27 May 2006), 18.

They called in close air support which launched missile strikes on buildings said to be occupied by Taleban fighters. One missile hit a school. The US forces said afterwards that seven people were killed. For two weeks they rejected the claims of UN and NGO workers that at least 70 were killed, and probably up to 90. And for two weeks that official US position held unchallenged.

Then, unexpectedly, in early September grainy mobile phone video emerged from this Third World village of traditional mud huts. It claimed to show up to 90 bodies laid out under blankets, apparently victims of the air strike.[66] At a stroke the video seemed to make vulnerable the US commander's original position. In the public domain it immediately suggested an active policy decision by the military to cover up the true civilian cost of the operation. Four-star US general, David McKiernan had known no details of the incident. His staff had not thought it necessary to refer them up to him, But the combination of pressures and questions suddenly forced the details on to his desk belatedly. They then obliged the general to issue a statement that 'in the light of emerging evidence' he was requesting a commander from outside the Afghanistan US command to review the incident. McKiernan repeated that this was 'in respect to the new evidence'. In other words, the US military's own initial After Action Report had seen no need to give ground to outside claims, and to investigate further. Only the video from one most unlikely 'information doer' with a mobile phone who happened to be present at the incident had forced an investigation where otherwise it must be assumed there would have been none.

The subsequent investigation traced a total of eleven videos of the event. It concluded that 55 people were killed, not the seven as claimed officially after the incident. Of the number killed, 33 were civilians and 22 'Anti Coalition Militants' (ACMs). It conceded there had been 'investigative shortfalls' and recommended more comprehensive, timely investigations. But it concluded that 'the validity' of other investigations that originally suggested 90 victims was 'in question'. Other evidence was 'tainted by alleged witnesses' interests in seeking financial, political, and/or survival agendas'.[67]

Subsequently it emerged that the military's significant under-reporting of deaths for two weeks was – as one source put it – because 'the system did not provide data to McKiernan' due to what are 'still very big institutional and cultural resistances inside the military'. Internal resistance came from the 'cultural hangover that everything is meant to be classified' which in turn is due to 'short term institutional old think' by information handlers. This was despite standing procedures under the NATO Military Committee's

[66] Tom Coghlan, 'Harrowing Video Film Backs Afghan Villagers' Claims of Carnage Caused by US Troops', *The Times* (8 Sept. 2008).

[67] Executive Summary dated 1 Oct. 2008 of the US AR 15-6 Investigation signed by Brig. Gen. Michael W. Callan.

MC 457 instructions that public information is a 'command responsibility of the highest priority', that 'maximum information' must be given to the public and the 'public should not be deprived of facts', that 'declassification of information [is] essential for public support and understanding', and that 'lack of information from official sources could lead to a loss of credibility'.

Many weeks after the US military investigation was published, the grainy video continued to provide grounds to challenge the credibility of the military conclusions. In January 2009, five months after the incident, Human Rights Watch made a reassessment of the evidence from Azizabad and labelled the published military inquiry 'deeply flawed' because of a methodology that presumed large numbers of dead were insurgents and that graves only contained one body.[68]

Together, this handful of examples confirms a clear trend. Almost by the day, these new real-time information realities are 'lighting up' the resistances within institutional systems to handle them. Backed by a robust, Bush-era political line defined in Washington as unsympathetic to new media realities, an ingrained US military culture even tried to pay media to plant good news stories.[69] Worldwide such official disrespect for the shifting information landscape is widespread. As confirmed by the work of campaigning journalism groups like the International News Safety Institute, Reporters Without Borders and the Rory Peck Trust, the issue continues to generate latent fears around the world for the basic rights of those who bear witness with their pocket technologies. But why is it that even with this relentless pressure the official mind-walls are nowhere close to beginning to crumble? The 'courtiers [in government systems] like behaviour that masks the truth' was how one former senior government figure described institutional reactions to the new reality. They tend to 'ratchet up old means of control' rather than embracing new liberating principles.

The working assumption now must be that *news* and *truth* merge far more swiftly than assumed, even if this real-time process happens imperfectly and does not always turn out to be the case. In the past the recording and global availability of images used to be limited and uncertain. It might have taken weeks, days or – more recently – hours to emerge. This often gave officials the relative luxury of time to gather data and ponder what public line to put out, often on their own terms. Now the time between the moment of crisis and the proliferation of graphic information launched digitally into the public domain can be measured in minutes, and is preciously short. The assumed luxury of that 'ponder time' at all levels has been eliminated.

[68] Human Rights Watch, 'Afghanistan: US Investigation of Airstrike Deaths "Deeply Flawed"', New York, 15 Jan. 2009.

[69] Jamie Wilson, 'Pentagon Pays Iraqi Papers to Print its "Good News" Stories', *Guardian* (1 Dec. 2005).

It would be wrong to give the impression of total official ineffectiveness or a blanket official inability to embrace the tyranny of the new real-time media challenge. There are some first signals of an official awareness of recognising the need to come to terms with the latest stage in the shifting realities of power.[70] In late 2007, NATO showed belated signs of not just reluctantly accepting but confronting the acute pressures on policy from the new media transparency. Because of the increasingly negative public perceptions of its operations to eliminate the Taleban threat in Afghanistan, the very credibility of the Afghan mission among the electorates of up to 40 contributing nations was on the line. Politically and militarily there was growing exasperation at the alliance's inability to counter the inevitably negative impressions of frequently successful operations. Political approval and funding were needed for a radical overhaul in handling public information (PI). So the Secretary General Jaap de hoop Scheffer went public. 'The media environment is changing in fundamental ways', he warned a NATO PI conference held specifically to coordinate the case for a more assertive approach. 'We are fighting with one arm behind our back. The other is pretty weak too,' he conceded. Most significantly he added: 'We are paying a price for it'.[71]

A few days later the alliance's defence ministers enhanced the PI budget by millions of euros. The limited amount of new money bought greater understanding and impact as opposed to just an increased human and technical capacity to change public perceptions. 'We dragged ourselves from the 1900s to 1970s' one official said wearily. It generated a new ability for NATO to 'get round journalists'. After 'huge fights' it broke the chain of command with a 'cultural shift on information sharing' that allowed speedier handling of crisis information. There was a new challenge to 'cultural hangovers that everything is meant to be classified'.

Yet there was much still to change and improve. By and large, NATO mindsets remain in a 'totally different field' to those of enemies like the Taleban. 'Old media' perceptions continue to be the assumption and 'we are still not using the right metric'. This meant that into 2009 little had improved substantively, despite the Secretary General's public warning eighteen months earlier. There were continuing national resistances to NATO's new, and radical, Strategic Communication Policy that was tabled in November 2008 and was designed to be effects-based.

The strongest objections to this radical overhaul came from the United States. On the day he entered office, President Obama seemed to signal a new

[70] See an official awareness of new levels of public empowerment in remarks by David Halpern, Director of the Strategy Unit in the UK's Cabinet Office, quoted in Patrick Wintour, 'Ministers Wake to Potential of People Power on the Net', *Guardian* (10 Feb. 2007), 16.
[71] On the record remarks to a NATO internal conference on Public Information in the Danish Foreign Ministry. 9 Oct. 2007

lawful and moral approach beyond Bush's previous adherence to a narrow national selfishness. Obama made a point of challenging head-on what much of the world viewed as the Bush era's hypocritical assumptions on values and moral obligations. He told the worldwide audience for his inauguration: 'our [US] power alone cannot protect us, nor does it entitle us to do as we please'.[72] It was hoped that this included official US appreciation for the policy implications of the new media landscape. But in the first weeks there were no reasons for optimism.

Up to that moment the US had not been alone in its institutional arrogance towards the rights of many, including the information doers. There was a similar – if extreme – audit of the cost of failing to embrace the new realities from the activities of Burma's military junta. But unlike NATO, the junta remained dismissive and in denial about the implications of the scale of media change underway.

During the sudden wave of mass pro-democracy protests against it in September 2007 the Burmese junta described as a 'skyful of lies'[73] the explosion of vivid digital content beamed out of internet cafes and on mobile phones that revealed the scale of street demonstrations. This ominously loaded description was the most dramatic institutional rejection of the new reality.

Such colourful rhetoric could easily be written off as merely the outrageous rantings of a brutal, authoritarian regime. That would be wrong. That almost delicious but disparaging phrase 'skyful of lies' neatly captures in a more extreme way the kind of instinctive, dismissive epithets used by many civil servants, political leaders, senior military officers and corporate executives in response to the acute pressures brought on by a sudden, unexpected crisis. It encapsulates the pressures of the moment when there is routinely a torrent of public digital information that swiftly paralyses the ability of political and corporate decision-makers to act decisively and wisely. It also identifies the visceral dismissal by institutional thinking of the dramatic unfolding realities for which their minds and systems have never been prepared adequately.

So the new core challenge is the Tyranny of the Time Line. Government and corporate institutions need to understand that this is a fundamental shift in media dynamics.

[72] Inauguration address on 20 Jan. 2009: www.whitehouse.gov/blog/inaugural-address/

[73] Editorial in *New Light of Myanmar,* an official newspaper of the junta (27 Sept. 2007). It said: 'Certain western media and anti-government media are broadcasting leading news stories and distorted news stories to stir up the mass protest . . . Now the majority of people who want to lead a peaceful life and are in favour of transition to democracy in a smooth way are gradually suffering from the evil consequences of the protests.'

5. First, fast, flawed and frightening: the tyranny of the time line

In one of my first studies[74] in the mid-1990s I warned of the looming 'Tyranny of Real Time' because of the 'cruel and arbitrary' pressures likely to be imposed on policy-makers by dramatic, if as yet indefinable, technological changes. To that tyranny must now be added a second: the new 'Tyranny of the Time Line'. In policy terms this can be equally cruel and arbitrary.

In crisis management presentations to professional audiences of policy-makers, military or corporate executives who are expected to have a worldly, informed perspective, I routinely identify these two tyrannies of the information space. I underline how there is no other option but to embrace them robustly with unhesitating commitment following a moment of sudden, massively destabilising shock that is created by the unexpected. Together, these two tyrannies create the new pinch point of tension.

Why is this? Most critically, the time lines of media action and institutional reaction are out of sync. The information pipelines facilitated by the new media can provide information and revelations within minutes. But the apparatus of government, the military or the corporate world remain conditioned to take hours.

In the mid-1990s, as these new pressures grew, policy-makers, commanders and corporate executives could remain defiant. They could hide under the old comfort blanket of slower reaction time guaranteed by distance, technological limitation and the natural assumptions of institutional power. As a result they largely believed that the 'dangers of false response are overstated, or at least that the time pressures inherent in real-time television can be managed'.[75] While there was once a common assumption that real-time coverage – once labelled

[74] Gowing, *Real-Time Television Coverage.*

[75] Warren Strobel, *Late-Breaking Foreign Policy* (Washington, DC: US Institute of Peace Press, 1997). See the chapter 'Driving Fast Without a Road Map' esp. p. 81.

the CNN effect – created an imperative that 'something must be done', often that 'something' was an active decision to do nothing or as little as possible, with a good chance of getting away with it.[76]

Ten years ago the typical institutional assumption was of a relatively leisurely period of up to 24 hours to gather data internally and then respond publicly.[77] By around 2005, the time created by the new realities of the real-time tyranny had probably shrunk to between two and four hours.[78] By 2009 my analysis is that the time available is down to no more than a few minutes, although maybe one hour or occasionally two if luck is on the institution's side.

That very short time frame is critical. The knee-jerk value judgement by many officials on whether this is a good or bad thing is irrelevant. Such are the technological realities that this is what it must be assumed to be. Those few minutes define the ever more voracious but limited information space which is open to be filled immediately after the start of any crisis. And the race to fill it[79] is vicious, with acute tensions between media players and policy responders which one senior minister candidly described as 'quite mad'.

Natural assumptions by leaderships that their *ex-officio* powers mean they will inevitably control this space as of right are grossly misplaced.[80] Insiders confirm that to marshal information and prepare an accurate, considered, official response is 'a helluva lot to ask for in two hours'. But to fail to produce anything for public consumption means an ever higher cost for the credibility of policy-makers. This is why institutionally there remains such an 'immense burden of accountability' on ministers especially. Insiders confirm that many officials 'are still afraid that entering the [post-crisis information] space is a career risk' because of the 'fear of errors' or giving a factually flawed briefing. In multiple government departments there is 'still reluctance to understand the relevance of information'.

[76] Gowing, *Real-Time Television Coverage.*

[77] For example, during the Kosovo war in 1999, a NATO air strike mistakenly hit a bus crossing the Luzane bridge outside Pristina on 1 May. The first AFP news agency report of the incident at 1348 confirmed that 23 people had been killed. A second report at 1357 confirmed that an 'AFP reporter at the scene . . . was able to see the bodies of victims'. At the daily NATO briefing twenty minutes later at 1415, the first reports of the incident were put to NATO spokesman Colonel Konrad Freitag. Unsighted and taken aback by what was being reported to him he responded to journalists: 'I don't have any evidence of this kind of accident. But I will check and come back on that tomorrow' – which would mean 24 hours later. 'Have you seen that report?' he was asked. 'No I have not seen that report.' But by this time the news agencies and channels were already buzzing with vivid details of an apparent NATO targeting disaster. These were defining public perceptions instantly. NATO took no position of any kind in the crisis space – except silence.

[78] See the details in this Chapter of official response times after the multiple bomb attacks on London's transport system on 7 July 2005.

[79] The concept of 'Race for Space' at the start of a crisis emerged in private, unattributable conversations I had with the British army commander General Sir Rupert Smith while he was still serving. He has since referred to the principle of the concept and the implications in his book *The Utility of Force: The Art of War in the Modern World* (London: Penguin-Allen Lane, 2005), 391-4.

[80] For a more detailed discussion of this shortcoming see 'Crisis and Time Urgency' in Nye, *Power to Lead*, 102–5.

The unexpected experience of the BBC and many major British media organisations in the hours after the tube and train bombings in London on 7 July 2005 confirms both the tyrannical nature of the time line and the almost merciless, competitive rush to fill the media space. In one way or another all of them were caught wrong-footed and ill-prepared. 'I have never experienced anything like this before. The bar has been raised suddenly' said one source. For the first three hours, the official government line reflected the view of Transport for London that the incidents – however deadly – were somehow due to a catastrophic 'power surge'. But within the first 80 minutes in the public domain there were already 1,300 blog posts[81] signalling that explosive devices were the cause. Like all news outlets, BBC News was overwhelmed by eye witnesses confirming that bombs had destroyed the trains and bus, and that there had been significant casualties. The content of the real-time reporting of 20,000 emails, 3,000 text messages, 1,000 digital images and 20 video clips was both dramatic and largely correct. All traditional news outlets experienced a similar deluge of postings.

In comparison, the official government capability in that first three hours was well behind the curve and inadequate. It took one hour to convene the government's COBRA crisis management cell, then longer to review the torrent of data coming in from the various civil and security agencies. This included first urgent assessments of whether there were chemical, biological, radiological or nuclear traces at any of the four incident locations, three of them in appalling, almost inaccessible tunnel locations underground. 'I was just desperate for clarity,' said one of those present. One senior police commander confirmed how he turned to TV channels as he sought greater real-time accuracy on what was unfolding. On many issues the rolling news coverage was broadcasting a stream of more relevant perspectives than the police force's Gold commander. The official challenge was to have 'a discipline to say you do not know' at such a critical time when the 'responsibility of government is to be factually correct'. This meant that the government could not reliably fill the post-crisis information space anything like as fast as the information doers. It also added to the concerns of a deeply nervous public about the extent of official government grip on the crisis.

Within two hours, the Metropolitan Police Commissioner, Sir Ian Blair boldly took the risk of taking on the tyranny of the time line. He decided to reject the cautious advice of his communications team not to go public.[82] Just after 11 am he appeared live on TV networks to declare that London was safe. This was despite what could easily have been the reality of a second or third

[81] www.technorati.com

[82] Confirmed in quotes from Sir Ian Blair in Ian Katz, 'The Year of Living Dangerously', a profile of his first year in office, *Guardian* (30 Jan. 2006).

wave of bombings that would have discredited instantly his reassurances.

That dilemma and decision confirmed the fundamental central concern: when to take on the tyranny of the time line and intervene with real-time information, even if it is incomplete, possibly flaky and probably cannot be verified with 100 per cent accuracy? Routinely I detail in presentations the identical dilemma faced by newsrooms, cabinet crisis cells and corporate board rooms alike as the time line ticks from zero through the first minutes towards the first and second hours. The information handling dilemmas converge under the challenge of F3. You can be *First*, and you can be *Fast*. But in entering the race for the information space how *Flawed* – how mistaken and inaccurate – might you be?

Despite the acute F3 dilemma, the imperative for official or corporate institutions to fill that space somehow is now almost extreme. But this is when it is clear that most still do not have the appropriate mindset to cope. These institutional shortcomings, resistances and reluctances were vividly highlighted when I detailed the dilemma during one off-the-record speech to a large gathering of very senior civil servants and security officials from several northern European countries. The head of one prime minister's private office confirmed the scale of the mind-walls and institutional vulnerabilities when he expressed formal thanks at the end of the presentation. Adapting the 'F3' analysis I had just outlined, he expressed appreciation for my 'Factual' and 'Forceful' analysis. Then, speaking for all senior officials in the room, he added: 'but for all of us, the new media reality you highlighted was above all *Frightening*!'

The phrase 'but . . . above all frightening!' confirmed the nature and scale of the vulnerability for policy-makers that this study is seeking to explore and define. So did the nervous laughter of mostly very senior colleagues as they realised how their own institutional inadequacies were being exposed.

This experience is often repeated when I identify F3 – frequently too often. Yet to realise such shortcomings and inadequacies in moments of crisis is a first stage for policy-makers in coming to terms with vulnerabilities they had largely not recognised until now, for whatever reason. The volunteering of the word 'frightening' was a candid and important confirmation of how far existing institutional systems and attitudes are out of sync with the often breathtaking time-line pressures and new information realities. Together they have created a new visibility that both challenges and threatens institutional competence because of 'new forms of action and interaction' that are frequently generated.[83] In the new tyranny of the time line, instant public perceptions

[83] John B.Thompson, 'The New Visibility', *Theory, Culture and Society*, 22/6 (2005), 31–51, highlights the 'new world of mediated visibility'; also Andrea Brighenti, 'Visibility', *Current Sociology*, 55/3 (2007), 323–42, confirms the new cutting edge status of the concept 'visibility' by asking if it should be recognised as a 'general category for the social sciences'.

and spontaneous opinions are created rapidly in minutes, even if information is incomplete.[84] Any misperceptions which go uncorrected can often gain instant credibility. Then they are impossible to reverse and therefore become distorted, sometimes with devastating repercussions for official reputations and integrity.

This creates a fundamental imperative. Whether the institutional or corporate culture feels comfortable with it or not, the duty must be to act assertively and swiftly to fill the space, however briefly or incompletely. As shown by that cautious advice from senior officers and communications advisers to Metropolitan Police commissioner Blair immediately after the 7/7 London public transport bombings, there usually remains a deep institutional resistance towards being forced to feed the news beast. But the acute pressure, especially at the start of the crisis, will not evaporate or disappear, however strong the will that it should. The 24/7 news environment will not suddenly vaporise conveniently either. Nor will the new breed of 24/7 technologies suddenly and miraculously be disinvented. Even if the emerging picture is thin and far from complete, the assumption must be that in some imperfect way it is conveying instant truths. So the imperative must be to enter the information space swiftly and report whatever is clear and known, however little that is. Yet the instinctive official and bureaucratic reaction remains one of holding back from any rapid response. The assumption is that the accuracy of facts and respect for the next of kin are the priority. However, while these are admirable principles to try to uphold, the price paid if nothing is said is even greater. It is preferable to say something brief and unambiguous rather than leave a void to be filled by bloggers, speculation and allegations that fast become impossible to reverse.

There are two vivid examples of the impression left by failing to embrace what many will still view as this unpalatable reality of the time line.

Two days after he was re-elected in November 2004, President George Bush held a press conference at the White House[85] to celebrate his victory and to highlight hopes for his second four years in office. At the time, the Palestinian president Yasser Arafat was in intensive care and close to death at a military hospital outside Paris. As the President came to the end of outlining

[84] There is now an overwhelming number of examples. (A) In the campus shootings at Virginia Tech University in the US on 17 Apr. 2007, mobile phone footage of the first shootings by a deranged Korean student was circulating and available to mainstream news outlets almost before the killer began his second round of shootings two hours later. The public media space had a clearer perception of what was taking place than the campus police and authorities. They were so shocked by the incident and its scale that they had difficulty mobilising a capacity to respond to a major crisis they had never expected. (B) When on 30 June 2007 two men attacked Glasgow airport's main terminal building in a car packed with gas cylinders, video taken by a passenger of the attack and resulting fires was swiftly circulating in the media space while police and the emergency services were still trying to bring the incident under control. The graphic video even included a shot of one severely burned bomber (who later died) with police standing over him.

[85] 4 Nov. 2004.

one element of his future policies, a news agency wire flashed an unsourced report that Arafat had died. One of the correspondents in the briefing room had seen the report. He was able to get Bush's attention and be recognised to ask the first question.

'Thank you, Mr President. I know you have not had a chance to learn this. But it appears that Yasser Arafat has passed away. . .'

'Really,' said Mr Bush looking suddenly most uncomfortable.

' . . . and I was just wondering if I could yet your initial reaction, and also your thoughts, perhaps, on working with a new generation of Palestinian leadership'.

The President started nodding and grimacing. He anxiously looked back and forth around the room. 'I appreciate that. My first reaction is God bless his soul. My second reaction is that . . .'

At this point the President faltered looking lost for thoughts and words. At this point too, audiences of senior political figures, civil servants or corporate executives to whom the clip is shown usually start sniggering. It is any official's nightmare, and they relate personally to the president's public dilemma.

Without any briefing or advance warning about Arafat's condition, the President had been wrong-footed. He stumbled as he tried to recall and restate US policy. Viewers could imagine the sudden anxiety of nervous officials in the wings. Might the President mis-speak, with complex political repercussions across the Middle East? He muddled through – just about. Then he looked down in a somewhat shell-shocked way before eventually asking for another question. At this point the audiences of high-level policy-makers often snigger again.

To recall this incident is not to revel in a President's misfortune. It is designed to highlight the tyrannical impact of the hyper-short time lines created by the new global information flows and the policy vulnerability which it creates. Even the President and commander in chief of the world's superpower could appear destabilised by the speed of information that the massive US government system could not log and process in time. On this occasion that was reinforced four minutes later when the live BBC World News transmission cut back to me in studio. I had to correct the President by quoting French military officials in Paris. They had just responded to the news agency report and Bush's reaction by confirming that Arafat was not dead!

The second of what could be many examples of a real-time information vulnerability at the highest level was during the 2006 Lebanon war with Israel. With hostilities continuing, Lebanese Prime Minister Fouad Siniora addressed a press conference at the end of a meeting of Arab League foreign ministers in Beirut which pressed the UN to draft what became resolution 1701 for a post-war Lebanon.[86] He emotionally listed the impact of Israeli attacks on cities and 'dozens of other villages and towns'. He then suddenly added to his list: 'The latest of which was an hour ago. The horrific massacre in the southern village of Houla that resulted in more than forty martyrs following Israeli raids and air strikes.'

Mr Siniora was quoting information reaching him from within an administrative structure wracked and exhausted by almost a month of war. The prime minister will have repeated in good faith the information that was handed to him about 'forty martyrs'. But for whatever reason it was wrong and behind the information curve.

Had the message become garbled? Was there propaganda mischief in the minds of some of his officials or those that served him? That is unlikely. And the explanation is really not so relevant. What was important was the perception left by a prime minister reporting grossly inaccurate information. Within an hour the number of deaths was reduced officially from forty to one.

The massive discrepancy left a suspicion – no doubt wrong – that the prime minister had willingly been part of a policy to exaggerate the impact of Israeli military attacks. He had been 'first' and 'fast'. He had decisively entered the post-crisis information space. But the reputational price paid was that his information had been 'flawed'. He had failed the F3 test. The Arab League meeting was a high-profile opportunity to display statesmanship in a crisis. But he should not have risked sullying his reputation with inaccuracies at a time when securing international support and credibility was of paramount importance to his country's fragile government. He should have been advised to wait and be sure of the numbers.

Both the Bush and Siniora examples highlight a critical disconnect in this new dynamic. It is between the impact of instant coverage, the context in which what is taking place is set, and the systemic disciplines needed to handle the whole process. This is especially because of the impact of video. 'Images bugger things up when there is no context' was one appropriate description during the brainstormings for this study. Fundamentally this observation is nothing new. What is new is the fiendishly short time line now created for institutional reaction. Graphic real-time images often alert policy-makers, the media and the world before the highest official levels even know that something has taken place. In doing so they only portray with good real-time accuracy a partial truth of what is taking place. The images usually come first. Reporting to confirm, explain and provide the critical factual detail will come many minutes or even hours later. Critically this can mean that context and perspective are in short supply until it is far too late on the time line. On

[86] 7 Aug. 2006, 1150 GMT.

most occasions, however, the level of accuracy – and therefore truth – can be breathtakingly high.

Such systemic weaknesses are exposed in even more damaging ways if there is internal institutional incompetence or – worse still – active official obstruction or indifference to ensuring the pressures of the time line.

The botched police handling of the mistaken shooting of the Brazilian electrician, Jean Charles de Menezes, at Stockwell underground station in the emotionally charged atmosphere fifteen days after the 7 July 2005 London transport bombings highlights this. For many reasons the de Menezes case is both a tragic and extreme example of the instant reputational price paid for filling the post-crisis space with inaccurate, incomplete and ultimately manipulated information. Yet it is emblematic of the core institutional weakness as the eventual report of the Independent Police Complaints Commission confirmed,[87] this predicament was made even worse by internal official rivalries. They meant that the officer with ultimate responsibility, Commissioner Sir Ian Blair, was actively denied vital real-time information about an operational failure by the senior commander reporting to him, Assistant Commissioner Andy Hayman.

In a press briefing at 1539 on 22 July, a few hours after the incident, Sir Ian Blair said the shooting was 'directly linked to the ongoing and expanding anti-terrorist operation'. Blair's words left a clear impression in the public mind that de Menezes was a bombing suspect. Yet by that time in the middle of the afternoon both senior commanders and more junior Scotland Yard staff knew a terrible error had been made. Off-duty officers watching cricket at Lords, some government officials, Sir Ian's Chief of Staff and even secretaries knew there had been an operational 'cock-up'. Assistant Commissioner Hayman also had doubts, based on a driving licence, Inland Revenue documents and other identification evidence found on the body. At 1630 Mr Hayman even briefed crime correspondents that the shot man was 'not' or 'not believed to be' a suspected bomber. However this doubt was not passed on to the Commissioner a few minutes later at the routine 1700 office meeting. The impression left overnight was that Blair continued to believe de Menezes was a legitimate terrorist suspect.

Subsequently there were widespread public suspicions that Blair had authorised and led a cover up. The IPCC report concluded he had not. Instead it asked why had 'the commissioner remained uninformed of key information . . . until next day'. It concluded that Mr Hayman had 'deliberately withheld vital information' and 'chose to mislead' both the public and Sir Ian. Mr Hayman continues to reject this IPCC contention. Most relevant for this

[87] For full analysis and detail to confirm this, see the 2nd report of the Independent Police Complaints Commission, 2 Aug. 2007: www.ipcc.gov.uk/news/pr020807_stockwell2.htm

discussion paper is Sir Ian's reflection two years later on what he was told, not told and why. At the press conference on 2 August 2007 for the IPCC report's publication he said: 'Few organisations would not be found wanting in such circumstances, particularly in relation to communication.' This is a profoundly important confirmation of the new vulnerabilities and fragilities for any institution inherent in a real-time crisis. In this case they were multiplied by personnel clashes[88] during what Commissioner Blair later described as 'the most testing operational challenge the service has faced since the second world war'.[89] Central reasons for it being so testing were core issues relating to the inadequate real-time handling of vital operational information.

The de Menezes case highlights what can be the tragic reputational price paid because of both systemic and cultural inadequacies. And they remain commonplace across a vast range of policy-making institutions. The de Menezes case also highlights the fine line between successful and disastrous responses to the new media pressures by the same senior executive or commander.

Commissioner Blair had been praised fifteen days earlier, immediately after the London bombings on 7 July, because of the way he defied internal advice, swiftly entered the information space and declared the capital safe. Yet over the mistaken de Menezes shooting two weeks later the same commissioner and same force were censured for their messy, and many would say disgraceful, handling of real-time details.

Similar failures in handling internal communications under acute real-time pressures led to humiliation for the corporation that owned the Sago mine in the US state of West Virginia after 13 miners were trapped underground on 2 January 2006. In the understandable real-time rush to fill the post-disaster information space with what appeared to be good news, the state governor and mining company both compounded the public perception of professional incompetence. Tragically, their willingness to believe what turned out to be a garbled, misheard message from underground, is a familiar example of how – despite best intentions – those with senior executive responsibility can easily make overoptimistic assumptions and fall victim to the tyranny of the time line.

[88] An inquiry later cleared Sir Ian Blair of misconduct. Mr Hayman eventually retired from the force after issues relating to separate matters.

[89] Part of Sir Ian Blair's four-minute video to the Metropolitan Police on 22 Sept. 2008 on the day before the opening of the inquest into the de Menezes shooting. Blair also said the force's approach to the inquest 'will be one of humility': 'No one set out that day with any intent to let a young man die. The officers involved will be giving evidence of doing what they did with good intention. They have my support and should have yours. Nevertheless, this will be a difficult couple of months and we must brace ourselves for criticism.' On 12 Dec. the jury returned an 'open' verdict on how de Menezes died, having been instructed by the coroner that they could not return a verdict of 'unlawful' killing. The 'open' verdict was widely interpreted as meaning that the jury did not fully accept the police explanation that he was shot using techniques for an 'instant killing' because officers feared he would detonate a bomb.

Sago was the worst US mining disaster since 2001. The intense human drama of the small mining community inevitably commanded 24/7 media coverage. After 41 hours reporters quoted jubilant family members as being told by West Virginia governor Joe Manchin that 12 miners were alive. Manchin announced publicly: 'They told us they have 12 alive. We have some people that are going to need medical attention.'[90] The wives and families gathered in the Baptist church celebrated. They praised divine intervention. 'The Lord takes care of them', said one mother. Media organisations instantly broadcast the good news, and the first edition of the *New York Post* splashed 'Alive' across its front page.

For three hours families celebrated the rescue success. But during that time the rescue team had already told the mine management that all but one of the 13 miners were dead. At the church, Ben Hatfield, CEO of the International Coal Group, had to break the dreadful news to the families. He told them: 'there had been a lack of communication [with the rescue team]; that what we were told was wrong; and that only one [miner] survived'.[91]

Relatives were distraught. Fights broke out in the church and mine officials were attacked. The *New York Post* swiftly switched its front page headline from 'Alive' to 'Shock!' Inevitably the media were widely blamed for misreporting a rescue success. It was an easy accusation to make. But content analysis of hour by hour developments shows that in reality they had quoted family members and Governor Manchin whom they had to assume were accurately informed on what was happening underground. A short time later, Governor Manchin chose to be contrite and humble in public about the terrible errors in information. 'About the confusion, I can't tell you of anything more heart wrenching than I have ever gone through in my life. Nothing.' An emotional CEO revealed tearfully: 'It is sorrow beyond belief.

How did such a disastrous miscommunication happen? 'I can only say there was no one who did anything intentionally other than risk their lives to save their loved ones', said the governor.[92] Hatfield, the CEO, blamed the spread of the inaccurate report on 'miscommunication' between rescuers and the command centre that was 'overheard' by several people. A radio code had been misunderstood and passed on. He later told a press conference: 'They needed good information. And we were trying to get them good information. In the process of being cautious we allowed the jubilation to go on longer than it should have. That is just all I can say about it . . . !'

That terrible management dilemma at the Sago mine epitomises so many difficulties and challenges experienced by both governments and corporations

[90] AP wire at 0559 on 4 Jan.

[91] AP wire at 0816.

[92] AP wire at 1352.

of all sizes in handling real-time information. The mine management moved swiftly to fill the information space in good faith with what they believed was accurate information from rescuers underground. But then they were wrong-footed by the tyranny of the time line and all the classic dilemmas of 'F3' – First, Fast, but how Flawed? The initial handling of the numbers of dead was wrong. Apparent figures were not rechecked and confirmed before the mine management and governor Manchin happily revealed them. Then once the disastrous error was discovered, they hesitated for emotional and understandable reasons.

Both the handling of the de Menezes shooting by the Metropolitan Police and the handling of the West Virginia accident by the mine company and state governor are tragically all too typical. They highlight the brutal consequences and public costs of failing to embed robustly in systems the harsh operational implications of both the tyranny of real time and the tyranny of the timeline.

6. Fragmenting media space: the new asymmetric policy challenge from 'social media'

Since the harsh lessons from the July 2005 terror bombings in London, an exponential explosion of developments has sharpened the asymmetric information dynamic and the implications for policy-making.

The situation then is hard to recall or imagine now. For a start YouTube, Facebook, My Space, Twitter and Second Life did not exist. The spectrum of those who 'do media' in this new real-time information landscape is now almost infinite: from the bystander who suddenly becomes caught up in a crisis, to the insurgent with a deadly cause;[93] the private soldier in a trench trying to eliminate him, or the British ambassador addressing a video camera like a reporter during a picnic in the Panshir valley for the regular blog on his personal perspectives of Afghanistan.[94]

So in this new real-time information space it has to be asked: who now is a member of the media? The definitions are increasingly blurred and merging. For video, who is the TV correspondent? In an Afghan firefight is it Sean Langan, freelance TV reporter/producer? Or is it Guardsman Ryan Lloyd of 'C' Company, the Grenadier Guards? What is the difference? After all in different locations they are both seen[95] wearing body armour and Kevlar helmet lying on the ground dodging bullets and speaking to the camera about

[93] See the research work for the British MoD of Lt Cdr Steve Tatham (RN), Senior Research Fellow and Director Media, Communications and Political Inclusion Research, UK Defence Academy, Shrivenham, on the new asymmetric media challenges from insurgents: e.g. 'Countering Asymmetric Taliban Strategies in Afghanistan', at RUSI, London, 26 Mar. 2008. Also the work of John Mackinlay at the Insurgency Research Group based at Kings College, London: e.g. http://insurgencyresearchgroup.wordpress.com/2008/04/29/the-taliban%E2%80%99s-propaganda-of-the-deed-strategy/

[94] Sir Sherard Cowper-Coles (www.youtube.com/watch?v=MEzavsT1hP4), posted 5 Oct. 2007 officially via the British Foreign and Commonwealth Office.

[95] Example taken from video I use in presentations.

what they are witnessing and experiencing.

There must be a similar searching question for words and text. In a moment of crisis what is the difference – if any – between the staff reporter who observes, writes, blogs then files an article for an established media organisation, and the motivated amateur or quasi professional who does exactly the same for a web or blog site? Networking sites like Twitter, Facebook, My Space or ARRSE and Military.com, the unofficial rumour services for the British Army and the US military, have fast become the unmediated electronic scratch pads to which information doers instinctively default in order to share graphic information and images in a crisis. In the British forces in Afghanistan during 2008, commanders actively encouraged the development of blogging in words and video from the operational field, with certain conditions relating to operational security. The phenomenon has proliferated. Some of the enlightened commanders describe a much valued release valve for emotions and tensions, especially at the height of intense operations. While the military institutionally scorn 'the *meejah*', the new practising of basic media techniques of recording and online distribution have become a morale booster and operational crutch. Whether they realise it or not, they have made military personnel new 'information doer' members of the media. Officers report almost no resulting violations or operational anxieties. There is a centrality of appropriate self-restraint.

Do these sites and the increasingly prolific adventures into the media space have a critical mass to marginalise conventional broadcasting or print? Not yet. But that time may not be far away and is probably closer than most officials and executives are willing to contemplate or prepare for. Often the number of views or audience hits is tiny compared with the audience for traditional media platforms. Often, too, the content can be dull[96] or vacuous, even from the official sources who are under high-level instructions to make a fashionable information impact in this media space.[97] Are they yet the *Daily Me* envisaged by the information technology visionary Nicholas Negroponte in the mid-1990s?[98] Possibly, judging by the way 24/7 blogging in words and video[99] took on almost establishment status to rival traditional media during the 2008 US presidential election campaign.[100] But the explosion of unmediated use and sometimes unsubstantiated allegations have highlighted many unresolved

[96] See Justin.tv which focuses on 'lifecasting' and is designed to let anyone – described as The Crowd – supply the programming. It encourages a 'willingness to broadcast every moment of a person's everyday existence in real time'. The overall verdict is how dull it is. See Randall Stross, 'Web Shows that Test Limits of Boredom', *New York Times*, repr. *Observer* (21 Oct. 2007).

[97] See Helen Pidd, 'No.10 Goes Digital with a Spot of Twittery-Pokery', *Guardian* (18 Apr. 2008).

[98] Nicholas Negroponte, *Being Digital* (New York: Vintage Press. 1995).

[99] Gaby Wood, 'The You Tube Election: How the Internet is Changing the Rule of American Politics', *Observer* (8 July 2007).

[100] Brian Steller, 'Candid Cameras Transform US Campaign', *International Herald Tribune* (12 Feb. 2008).

negative issues.[101] This has included 'reporting' from frequently reliable blogs that was downright wrong because the 'reporter' had 'made it all up!'[102] So despite their pioneering and mass novelty impact, the current experimental variations of the blogging form still have to acquire a much clearer and more rigorous definition,[103] especially when it comes to their role in a crisis. That is unless they are catapulted into high-profile status by exposure on the more traditional media outlets.

There will continue to be long arguments over whether this new reality is citizen journalism, social media or another description. But the eventual tag is not so important. What is, is that it must be assumed that the nature of this ubiquitous and universally accessible media space is unforgiving, whatever the structures emerging. The content and its credibility are an additional complication in the post-crisis information space being contested. It is therefore vital to define and understand both the players operating in it and the implications for policy accountability. If they are not considered then there will be a professional price for both ignorance and naïveté that must be assumed to be witheringly high.

In this new asymmetric environment, for official systems there is now 'the sheer difficulty of getting absolute fact' under these ferocious pressures of the time line and the need to fill the media space. The broad challenges are identical, whether in the military theatre of battle, the crisis operational centre of a government, or the board room of a corporation. In a matter of minutes the images or words these new information players produce can be vacuumed up swiftly by the major traditional media outlets. There the unsolicited inputs are checked and processed into multiple versions by newsroom staff who are described by one *Economist* editor as *reportrons,* before they are transmitted on the organisation's multimedia platforms around the clock. This is how such real-time material becomes an instant lightning rod for a public passing of judgement on policy-makers. Whether fair or not, both can swiftly generate public perceptions of delay or prevarication that are often never reversed or corrected. There is also the expectation that 'if we are seeing it on TV, online, or on the web, then why aren't those in power acting fast to do something about it?'

This goes a long way to explaining two phenomena.

First, that low-level tactical incidents will often swiftly take on apparently strategic significance. Second, that local events will suddenly gain high-level international importance which is often not justified. Both can then be further

[101] Edward Luce. 'Online Obama Closes Net around Smears', *Financial Times* (13 June 2008).

[102] John Gapper, 'Shock: Drudge Loses his Grip!', *Financial Times* (30 Oct. 2008).

[103] For a taste of the debate underway see Danah M. Boyd and Nicole B. Ellison, 'Social Network Sites: Definition, History and Scholarship', *Journal of Computer-Mediated Communication,* 131 (2007), article 11: http://jcmc.indiana.edu/vol13/issue1/boyd.ellison.html

complicated by an additional destabilising factor for policy-makers. This is the 'burgeoning and highly polemical commentariat' that intervenes swiftly in print or online.[104] Their instant assessments can frequently polarise public views and perceptions even more sharply by drawing profound strategic conclusions from routine tactical setbacks which happen to be visually dramatic.

The attack on a British army Warrior armoured vehicle on a desert highway outside Basra on 19 September 2005 remains a classic example of all these disconnects of timelines, context and commentary.

A video camera was present when a crowd of Iraqis – later described by the British forces as 'violent and determined' – moved towards the Warrior. As well as rocks, they threw fire bombs and fired rockets which would normally just bounce off the armour. But this vehicle's optical sights were broken. So the crew had left open their steel hatch to facilitate navigation. A fire bomb struck lucky. It dropped through the open hatch and into the vehicle's crew space, instantly filling it with flames and smoke.

The camera which had been recording the crowd's attack then focused on the first crew member clambering out with his combat clothing on fire. As the Warrior driver frantically tried to manoeuvre back and forth to escape a crowd with the growing anger of a possible lynch mob, three more soldiers emerged from the turret apparently engulfed in flames.

The dramatic video was beamed worldwide within an hour via the Reuters agency feed.[105] The tactical predicament of one four-man Warrior crew instantly left an impression of a significant British military failure. The still images published on the main pages of internet sites and newspapers within hours left a similar impression. 'Torched' screamed the front page of the *Daily Mail* next day. Below the headline was the single image of an unnamed British squaddy. His helmet was on fire. His body was hunched with his back in flames. The Warrior's turret appeared to be well ablaze. Inside the *Mail* were another five pages of equally graphic images and coverage, with a second banner headline: 'Troops are Trapped in Legal Mire as the Hell of Iraq Explodes'.

But while vivid and compelling, the impression left in the first minutes and hours of coverage was misleading. It contained no context for what we later learned was a covert, dangerous and highly sensitive operation in which the Warrior had been involved and which had already been completed successfully. And the coverage could not confirm that remarkably all four crew members had survived and escaped with mostly light burns. One crew member was

[104] *How Much do Commentators Influence Politics and Public Opinion?* (London: Editorial Intelligence and Reuters Institute, 2008): http://reutersinstitute.politics.ox.ac.uk/fileadmin/documents/Publications/Power_of_the_Commentariat.pdf

[105] Item no. 130, 19 Sept. 2005. Duration 2'05.

evacuated back to hospital in the UK with 37 per cent burns. None of this could have been known when the video was swiftly aired. So the worldwide TV audiences knew nothing more and drew their own sombre conclusion.

Details of the British Special Forces operation would probably never have been released had the dramatic Warrior video not emerged in the real-time way it did. Unknown to anyone outside the British military command, two SAS troopers had been detained by Iraqi 'security forces' in the Jamiat police station. They had then been handed on to an illegal militia and were being held in a house. British commanders believed they faced death by summary execution.

Instant broadcasting of the graphic, uncut images of the mob attack on the Warrior suddenly created an unplanned, urgent imperative for public accountability during a covert operation. It forced the private office of the British Defence Secretary in London to become involved immediately. There would have to be a public statement. The driving principle was that: 'time is not the only priority, it is accuracy'. There was a realisation that 'if we get it wrong it can be a disaster'. So the private office bypassed the usual military hierarchy of reporting lines to demand details urgently from the operational theatre commanders, even though they were still preoccupied with the delicate rescue operation and safety of their troops.

Insiders later described a tense atmosphere, with the Secretary of State John Reid personally engaged in ways that were certainly most unusual for such operations. Unlike the US military's unwillingness to cascade vital real-time information to its four star general after the Azizabad bombing in August 2008, Reid demanded full details 'within thirty minutes to an hour'. His civil servants and military staff had been forced to wield at high speed the long policy-maker's screwdriver so often resented by commanders in the field. They were 'uncomfortable hours', one insider revealed. But there would have been no policy discomfort and no resulting public pressure for answers had the video of the Warrior in flames not emerged in the way it did, thereby highlighting the two 'cruel and arbitrary' tyrannies of real time and the time line at work in tandem.

While the video impression of military failure lingered for many hours, the Ministry of Defence confronted the need to explain the incident. It realised reluctantly it would have to release some level of fuller information about the safe rescue of the SAS soldiers in ways it had not planned for. How much detail should be confirmed? What about revealing identities? Should pictures of the two troopers manacled and cowering in the Iraqi police cell be publicised? Given the involvement of Special Forces and the British MoD's standing policy on never releasing details of SF operations or the identities of those involved, the decisions were complex. Unpixellated images of the two

SAS troopers manacled in the police cell were already circulating.

Much later that day, the MoD did choose to reveal enough details of the rescue operation to correct the wrong impression left in the first hours by the burning Warrior. The British force commander, Brigadier John Lorimer, released a carefully worded statement.[106] When photos were published, news organisations agreed to blur the faces of the soldier hostages to prevent identification.

Many hours after the incident, the MoD in London and the British forces in Basra had largely regained the high ground of information control. But only just. And the unjustified perception of an apparent military failure was never fully eliminated. This was compounded by coverage in British newspapers the next day. Alongside the graphic images of the soldiers in flames, came a procession of leading analysts – the commentariat – writing critically about the incident. They used the Basra events as a catalyst to highlight what they decided was the urgent need for a swift withdrawal from Iraq.

'When should we leave Iraq?' asked the London *Evening Standard*'s leader.[107] 'I've changed my mind on Iraq,' said the headline above an analysis by the military historian and journalist Sir Max Hastings: 'It is time to start talking about when and how we go', he wrote.[108] 'A fiasco without parallel. It is time to leave Iraq', wrote Sir Simon Jenkins in the *Guardian*,[109] which also headlined 'Softly, Softly Army Tactics Shattered by Day of Chaos'.

The real-time images of a tactical difficulty had suddenly – and typically – been escalated to apparently confirming a strategic policy vulnerability for the ministers and officials forced to handle it. It prompted the drawing of dramatic strategic lessons and conclusions out of all proportion to the tactical realities of the incident itself. As Brigadier Lorimer's statement said, the crowd of 200–300 was 'small' and 'unrepresentative' in a city of 1.5 million that was described as 'calm'.

Another prime example was video taken by a crew member on board a German navy vessel during what became disastrous high-speed manoeuvres off Lebanon in April 2007. A compelling minute of imagery shows one frigate missing another before smashing into a second. The sailor who recorded it can never have expected that when he pressed the record button his camera would witness a dramatic and professionally embarrassing incident, let alone the worldwide distribution his video eventually secured. The images circulated rapidly not on traditional media outlets but web platforms like YouTube[110] and

[106] For the text of Brig. Lorimer's statement see www.guardian.co.uk/world/2005/sep/20/military.iraq Note the emphasis on the need to explain the context of the event.

[107] *Evening Standard* (20 Sept. 2005).

[108] *Daily Mail* (20 Sept. 2005).

[109] *Guardian* (21 Sept. 2005).

[110] www.youtube.com/watch?v=Ib43gpKTxjs posted on 18 June 2007.

Blinkx.[111] Unlike the other 35 German naval incidents that took place in 2007, the public circulation of the Lebanon video produced inevitable pressure on the German Defence Ministry to account for the incident and be seen to take action. It did: it sacked the ship's captain rather than just discipline him. The public circulation of the video forced the ministry to take tougher disciplinary action than might otherwise have been the case. The response of Captain Götz Meiert, a German Navy spokesman, could be described as matter of fact after the enforced public profile generated by the YouTube posting. 'It's not a good record. But the point was that last year there were spectacular crash images which were spread by the media,' he told the Guardian, in language of denial which irrationally suggested the media were the problem. 'The number of accidents wasn't particularly high in total.' He then added fatalistically: 'It's bothersome that such things happen – but they do.'[112]

It is equally 'bothersome' when personal indiscretions are recorded privately by 'information doers' in an official position of responsibility, and then become public. The issues are usually inconsequential for official policy and strategy, but can be deeply embarrassing for perceptions. But they are like dynamite if the video is made for fun by a 'doer' like Britain's Prince Harry who is a serving junior officer in the British army, and records allegedly racist slurs about 'Pakis' and 'ragheads'. The passage of time does not diminish either the impact or obligation for accountability. Three years after shooting the video during army exercises in Cyprus, it emerged in Britain's *News of the World* under the headline 'Harry's Racist Video Shame', with three pages of detail and minutes of the video posted on the paper's website.[113] It became like an out-of-control flame thrower. The only practical official response was timely damage limitation. Despite a swift official apology from the prince, and MoD guidance that he would have a stern interview 'without coffee' with his commanding officer, the issues relating to military culture and British racist attitudes spiralled out of control. A predictable whirlwind of comment and complaint about a racist military culture forced the attention of ministers, royal aides, civil servants and military commanders alike. This was all because of a private video that contained an indiscreet description by a prince that somehow leaked and thereby highlighted the activities of an involuntary information doer.

Such asymmetric challenges coming from left field are not just troubling for the institutions of power. Traditional media organisations have to confront them suddenly too.

In the first two hours after the London tube and bus bombings on 7 July

[111] www.blinkx.com/video/german-navy-boats-crashing/YQb5P- NtWD0AVcvQppdnYA
[112] www.guardian.co.uk/world/2008/jan/30/germany.internet
[113] www.notw.co.uk (11 Jan. 2009).

2005 most media organisations were equally wrong-footed by the vast volume of digital information from amateur information doers that overloaded their newsgathering systems after just a few minutes. As already discussed, the torrent of data first surprised and then overwhelmed the capacity of many newsrooms to handle it. In the intense confusion there may have been exaggeration and double counting of some facts, but the overall trend was clear. The stream of data coming from the new generation of digitised bearers of witness was far more precise and consistent than anything the government and security services were in a position to reveal.

Most importantly, it had profound and irreversible implications for the real-time dynamics of newsgathering. The cutting edge experience during the London 7/7 bombings forced swift readjustments in traditional British news organisations. They nimbly assessed the implications of the new 'amateurs' doing media out there. There was also the need for timely newsroom procedures to validate what the amateurs said they had witnessed and recorded.

By 2008 news organisations of every kind had actively embraced the implications of the new phenomenon that swiftly became labelled User Generated Content. This was partly to improve real-time coverage of breaking news, and partly as a way to engage more actively viewers and readers because of the growing pressures on revenues, newsgathering costs and business models. Despite the price tag in additional personnel and systems costs, the news organisations embedded in newsrooms new mediating systems to cope with ever increasing flow of UGC material from a host of 'information doer' sources on multiple news stories that were often unfolding simultaneously.

The later warning from Sir Tim Berners-Lee, founder of the world wide web, that on these new platforms 'untruths start to spread more than truths',[114] or that the web is becoming a 'forum for conspiracy theories, rumour, innuendo and misleading information',[115] did not seem to apply in a major crisis. Far from it. The accumulated evidence is that the asymmetric torrent of overwhelming 'amateur' inputs from the new generators of content produces largely accurate, if personalised, information in real time. It may be imperfect and incomplete as the crisis time line unfolds. There is also the risk of exaggeration or downright misleading 'reporting'. But the impact is profound. Internal BBC research[116] discovered that audiences are understanding if errors or exaggerations creep in by way of such information doer material, as long as they are sourced and later corrected. It noted that 'rolling news that is "right at the time" is allowed

[114] Tim Berners-Lee quoted in the *Guardian* (3 Nov. 2006).

[115] See his comments in mid-Sept. 2008 on the eve of launching a new World Wide Web Foundation to investigate ways to police the accuracy of information on the internet. See http://news.bbc.co.uk/2/hi/technology/7613201.stm or 'The Web: Fact or Fiction Says Tim Berners-Lee' at www.guardian.co.uk/news/blog/2008/sep/15/timbernerslee.internet

[116] James Holden, 'A Creative Future for BBC Journalism', Oct. 2005: an audience research analysis undertaken by Sparkler for BBC MC&A.

[in order] to retain immediacy'. One viewer reflected the overall message: 'as long as they say it is unconfirmed it doesn't matter'. In addition, the concept of trust can 'flex' in a crisis. Trust does not diminish as long as the ongoing levels of doubt or lack of certainty are always made clear. It is about 'doing your best in [a] world where speed and information are the keys'. But the research concluded that the BBC needed to do more work to analyse the implications of the UGC phenomenon for accuracy, speed, personalisation, dialogue and trust. That challenge is the same for all traditional media organisations.

7. 'Bad apples' and 'failures in systems': the haunting pressure on credibility that never goes away

So a cheap, go-anywhere camera or mobile phone worth $300–$400 can challenge the credibility of the massive human and financial resources of a government or corporation in an acute crisis. It can also threaten to humiliate or bring to book leading figures in any public drama.[117] John B. Thompson concluded that the increasingly 'uncontrollable nature of mediated visibility' meant it was 'much more difficult to close the doors of the political arena and throw a veil of secrecy around it'.[118] But the response around government tables and in executive board rooms can still frequently seem to be similar to the experience of the legendary King Canute: like the incoming sea, the real-time information threat will not retreat as the courtiers believed it should because of their *ex-officio* powers.[119]

Case studies go a long way to confirming the nature of this institutional blindness and the new vulnerabilities of power it creates. Failures to embrace the tyrannies of real time and the time line mean that inevitably the list of examples is lengthening. Those that follow are chosen because they are both the most vivid and most emblematic of the systemic inadequacies they highlight.

[117] One example that highlights the principle in all parts of public life took place at the Japanese Formula 1 Grand Prix in Oct. 2007. A video taken from the crowd during a rainstorm showed the driver Lewis Hamilton apparently violating racing rules on one corner. A spectator had posted the video on YouTube in violation of F1 rules on broadcasting rights. It led to a stewards' inquiry on Hamilton's alleged erratic driving which could have meant disciplinary action. The video put Hamilton's image and reputation on the line. The inquiry cleared him.

[118] Thompson, 'New Visibility', 41 and 49.

[119] According to legend, the flattering courtiers of King Canute claimed he was 'So great, he could command the tides of the sea to go back'. But when they placed his throne on the beach, the incoming tide almost drowned him. In an alternative version of the legend Canute agreed to sit on the throne as the sea came in merely to prove how wrong his courtiers were!

Abu Ghraib: the 'trophy' photos that haunted the Bush administration

The credibility crunch becomes ever sharper for government and corporate reputations, if there are emotive, vivid images of casualties and bloodshed. This is borne out by the political impact of the revolting photos of naked Iraqi male prisoners inside Abu Ghraib prison outside Baghdad. But the political repercussions did not fade with time, They continued six years later.

The infamous digital images showed behaviour that no member of any armed forces should ever contemplate indulging in, let alone carry out. They were taken by the US soldiers Private Lyndy England and Sergeant Charles Graner between October and December 2003. In no way can it be argued that England and Graner were information doers with a quasi media role who sought to expose the abuse of prisoners. Not only had they been complicit in organising the horrific treatment of detainees. They had gone further and taken the images on a digital camera as private 'trophy' photos.[120]

The relevance of the Abu Ghraib photos for this discussion paper is in the lessons from the extraordinary political howlround and resulting pressure for high-level political accountability that exploded once the images leaked into the public domain. Photos taken casually for private purposes – albeit obscene – suddenly threatened the credibility of the most senior political and military figures in asymmetric ways that no one had ever thought possible. And pressure for accountability resulting from publication of those photos did not end with the Congressional hearings of 2004. It returned and continued years later at the end of 2008 in the final days of the Bush administration. A bipartisan Senate report[121] concluded that decisions by Defence Secretary Donald Rumsfeld in 2002 were a 'direct cause' of widespread detainee abuses. They were not due to 'a few bad apples' – junior soldiers – acting independently. There is a strong argument that this Congressional momentum to uncover what took place, and why, would never have happened without the public leaking of Graner and England's 'trophy' photos.

Once the nature of prisoner abuse became known to the Pentagon in late 2003, an official investigation was quietly ordered in January 2004. During its first weeks, the existence of the inquiry chaired by Major General Antonio Taguba was not revealed publicly. Nor was the fact that such unspeakable photos existed. But three months later the images leaked into the public domain. They first appeared on CBS's flagship TV programme *60 Minutes II* on 28 April. Then two days later the *New Yorker* website published a devastating

[120] For more details see e.g. Thomas E. Ricks, *Fiasco* (New York: Penguin Books, 2006), 378–80.

[121] Report of the US Senate Armed Services Committee inquiry into the treatment of detainees in US custody. Executive Summary published 11 Dec. 2008.

expose by the veteran investigative journalist Seymour Hersh.

The nature of the photos reflected catastrophically on a US global image that was already deeply scarred by the perceived failings of the Iraq war. The Arab and Muslim world was especially outraged. The accusations of complicity in the abuses by the Bush administration became unrelenting. Both the revelations about apparent Pentagon indifference and the resulting 'chattering and whispering campaign' in the White House became deeply damaging.[122]

Within days, the public circulation of the images created instant pressure for accountability at the highest levels of the Bush administration. General Richard Myers, Chairman of the Joint Chiefs, and General John Abizaid, Commander-in-Chief for Central Command, were leading names summoned by Congressional committees[123] to explain and defend the actions of the two low-level US soldiers on guard detail in Abu Ghraib. Senator Carl Levin feared the Graner/England pictures revealed an 'organised and conscious process of intelligence gathering'. He said that 'if true, the planners of this process are at least as guilty as those who carried out the abuses'.

This Congressional grilling in public that was sparked by the Graner/England pictures was humiliating for these public servants and senior commanders. They were even joined on Capitol Hill by Defense Secretary Donald Rumsfeld. He was seen being asked publicly by senators if he had considered resigning and taking personal responsibility for the leaked photos and breach of discipline codes. He accepted that it was a 'fair question' to be asked, and he had considered resignation. He also admitted that 'these events occurred on my watch', and that 'as Secretary of Defense, I am accountable for them, and I take full responsibility'. He then offered 'my deepest apology. It was inconsistent with the values of our nation and it was certainly fundamentally un-American.' General Abizaid was also seen voluntarily admitting to a string of failures. He spoke of 'failures in people doing their duty. There are failures in systems. And we should have known. We should have uncovered it, and should have taken action before it got to the point it got to.' None of this would have been forced into the public domain without the original Abu Ghraib pictures.

The issue of public accountability returned at the end of 2008. The report published by the US Senate committee[124] after it had conducted 70 interviews over 18 months, said blame was specifically not due to just 'a few soldiers acting on their own'. Pointing the finger at Defense Secretary Rumsfeld, it concluded that a series of high-level decisions in the Bush administration 'conveyed the message that physical pressures and degradation were appropriate treatment

[122] See Bob Woodward, *Bush at War Part III* (London: Simon & Schuster, 2006), 305–6.

[123] 7 May 2004.

[124] Senate report, 11 Dec. 2008.

for detainees in U.S. military custody'.

So six years on, the continuing accountability reverberations from the Graner/England private images confirm why their Abu Ghraib photos remain a prime example of the vulnerabilities for those in positions of power because of the new asymmetric impact of one single digital recording device. But the experience is not unique. Elements of the British forces operating in Iraq endured similar scrutiny in subsequent courts martial because of evidence of prisoner abuse that emerged by way of similar 'trophy' photographic imagery. The evidence and legal process tarnished the military's image. It also blighted both careers and professional reputations. As one senior security source put it: the mobile phone or digital camera in the webbing of a soldier fighting in Iraq or Afghanistan can suddenly make him or her a 'strategic private or corporal'. They can also record and reveal activities that are questionable, become issues for public debate and therefore have to be held to account.

Private Security Contractors: their activities exposed

Private corporations have equal vulnerability. The lucrative role of civilian Private Security Contractors (PSCs) in providing protection and escort duties to international forces in war zones has long been a controversial issue. For years their often armed personnel could operate with impunity. On occasions they suffered a terrible fate, as in Fallujah on 31 March 2004 when four contractors from the Blackwater corporation were videoed being dragged from a vehicle and bludgeoned to death before their bodies were set alight and hung from a bridge. Despite their often assertive use of weaponry and deadly force, the PSCs were accountable to the laws neither of the nation that hired them nor of the home nation the contractor organisation was operating from. In the majority of the 195 incidents between 2005 and 2007 where Blackwater employees fired their weapons in Iraq, they did so from moving vehicles without stopping to count the dead or assist the wounded.[125] A handful of governments like Britain had drafted 'green' discussion papers designed to create an eventual framework for legislation and oversight of PSC activities. But progress towards a new operating framework moved forward at barely a snail's pace, despite unrelenting pressure from NGOs and human rights groups. There were always suspicions that the legal no man's land in which PSCs operated was convenient cover for governments that needed to hire their services to increase security protection in the most hostile of environments.

A long string of questionable actions by PSCs in Iraq and Afghanistan

[125] Evidence assembled by the US House Committee on Oversight and Government Reform, 1 Oct. 2007.

never brought issues to the point where their future ability to operate was threatened. Then on 16 September 2007, armed Blackwater employees on a vehicle escort duty in central Baghdad shot dead at least 17 civilians who they claimed threatened them as they passed through the traffic intersection at Nissor Square. A key element of evidence collected against them by the increasingly assertive Iraqi government was video shot at the scene by an information doer. It was broadcast worldwide and immediately raised multiple questions about the Blackwater version of events and the credibility of what their contractors claimed took place. The video was a key reason for the political tide turning dramatically against the lack of accountability for PSCs, both in the country where they operated – like Iraq – and where their parent company was based – the United States. It also quickly carried a high commercial price in lost business.

Within a month, Blackwater's usually secretive co-founder and most senior executive Erik Prince was being grilled publicly by a US Congressional committee on his firm's 'aggressive and sometimes reckless record' which suggested his staff were trigger-happy 'cowboys'.[126] Within two months, US PSCs became subject to US military control, especially on the use of deadly force and all movements.[127] Within 16 months five Blackwater contractors were facing manslaughter charges in a US court,[128] a State Department advisory panel was recommending that Blackwater be dropped as a contractor for US diplomats in Iraq,[129] and from 1 January 2009 all PSCs became subject to Iraqi law with a new legal status that would remove any possibility of further cavalier behaviour with weapons. In mid-February 2009 Blackwater dropped all references to its now tainted name in order to remove the brand stain that had killed a lot of business. Blackwater Worldwide renamed itself Xe. Officially this was because the company said its focus was shifting away from the security contracting that had brought great wealth, but also tarnished its image. But the unexpected public visibility of the Nissor Square incident had exacted a corporate price. 'It's not a direct result of a loss of contract', a spokeswoman said of the name change. 'But certainly that was an aspect of our work we feel we were defined by', she conceded.[130]

So that single minute of information doer video evidence from 16 September 2007 had suddenly catalysed a process which first challenged the assumed inviolability of the PSCs, and then eventually reined in their activities. Over

[126] Brian M. Knowlton and John M. Broder, 'Blackwater Assailed at Hearing in House', *International Herald Tribune* (3 Oct. 2007).

[127] John M. Broder and David Johnston, 'Military to Oversee Security Contractors', *International Herald Tribune* (1 Nov. 2007).

[128] David Pallister, 'Foreign Security Teams to Lose Immunity from Prosecution in Iraq', *Guardian* (27 Dec. 2008).

[129] Associated Press, 17 Dec. 2008.

[130] Associated Press, 13 Feb. 2009.

the years most contractors had managed to see off growing pressures by using intense lobbying in Washington especially. Within days the video from the Baghdad incident had helped force them from their politically ring-fenced sanctuary into a process of accountability that left them vulnerable and their freedom of action greatly diminished.

Saddam Hussein's execution: the taunting that officials thought they had hidden

The way the Iraqi government ineptly and misleadingly handled the execution of Saddam Hussein on 30 December 2006 is another of the most graphic and sordid examples of how governments and anyone in the chain of official responsibility can be caught out.

Video taken on a mobile phone by an observer at the execution showed that the National Security Adviser, Mowaffak al-Rubai, must have knowingly lied in his public description of Saddam's final moments. During interviews immediately after the execution, Mr Al-Rubai calmly told BBC News and other international media that the process carrying out the death sentence had been 'calm, orderly and respectful'. There had been 'no taunting; no humiliation; no shouting match'. He added that 'all respect' was shown for the condemned man and there had been 'full respect' for international standards and Muslim ritual standards 'by the letter'. This impression was reinforced by the official release of a series of still photos of Saddam – with no sound track – being led to the gallows and the noose being put around his neck. There were also still images of the dead Saddam's head, shoulders and upper torso wrapped in a blanket

There had been no reason to question the official description of the execution by such a senior member of the Iraqi government. Around the world, international leaders welcomed the execution with restrained words that noted the event had taken place, along with remarks about the Iraqi legal process that had eventually brought him to the gallows.

But the official version stood for a few hours only. Its accuracy was challenged by shaky mobile phone video which quickly appeared on websites and DVDs in the Baghdad bazaar. Within a short time the imagery became available to news outlets worldwide. It told a dramatically different story. It showed that the National Security Adviser's version had to be both disinformation and probably a deceit. In reality, there had been taunting, humiliation and shouting that Al-Rubai said did not take place. Norms for an execution had been shown little respect.

It emerged that the government had allowed representatives of Saddam's

Shiite enemies to be part of the execution team. Followers of Muqtada al-Sadr taunted Saddam and hurled abuse. Guards shouted 'Muqtada! Muqtada! Muqtada!' Saddam was heard repeating the name sarcastically before shouting scathingly: 'Do you consider this bravery?' Some in the room reinforced the insults for Saddam, who was a Sunni. They recited the Shia version of an Islamic prayer. Then one yelled 'Go to hell!' A male voice said: 'Please, stop. The man is facing an execution.'

But to no avail. The video showed the trap door open. The crack of Saddam's snapping spine could be heard, and the former dictator was dead.

After the cell phone video emerged, political leaders around the world had to be approached again to be asked for their revised reaction to the true nature of the execution. In Britain several ministers in the Blair government united to use the same word to condemn the true process of the execution. It had been 'deplorable!'

Across Iraq there were fears that the leaked video would prompt new violence and further radicalise the already inflamed ethnic tensions, both within Iraq and across the Gulf region and Middle East. It would be 'extremely damaging' for Iraq's delicately balanced reconciliation efforts and the fragile coalition government. An adviser to the Prime Minister confirmed there would be an inquiry.[131] An official who had led the execution process was later arrested.

The issue is not the execution itself. It is the profound asymmetric impact of what the unauthorised 'one eye' on someone's mobile phoned recorded during Saddam's final moments, then what it revealed. It confirmed that in the intense emotion after the execution Al-Rubai had for some reason decided to mislead the Iraqi and global public about what really took place.

In Iraq the ineptitude of Al-Rubai's initial remarks could be put down to the understandable immaturity of post-Saddam governance structures, and to personnel who were still feeling their way. But they are not alone in trying to deceive and mislead in such a brazen, misguided way. The asymmetric power of a mobile phone's video lens and the impact of such political stupidity would be equally profound and troubling anywhere in the world. The European Union's Foreign Policy Coordinator Javier Solana drew an important lesson after the truth of Saddam Hussein's execution was revealed: 'That guy; that person who took that picture on the mobile telephone, and was transmitted to the Arab world, created an impact on the Arab world that he does not know . . . A picture can change the world much more than many speeches . . . It is a good lesson that we – politicians – have to draw.'[132]

[131] Ned Parker, 'Inquiry into Taunting of Saddam at his Execution', *The Times* (2 Jan. 2007).

[132] Remarks in an open discussion with David Ignatius, Associate Editor of the *Washington Post*, at the Brussels Forum of the German Marshall Fund on 27 Apr. 2007.

So why, then, do others at the highest levels of national power still fail to grip the implications of believing that in real time it is possible to distort reality and get away with it?

Iran: the real-time deceit that undermined its own propaganda push

In July 2008 Iran embarked on a new round of diplomatic brinkmanship over its assumed advanced work to build nuclear weapons. It decided to present the impression that it possessed a self-confident, functioning ballistic missiles programme. This in turn left open an unanswered question. Were the missiles seen being launched to great national celebration capable of carrying the kind of nuclear weapon which Iran always insisted it was not building? Then came a further mystery. Why did Iran risk the credibility of its case by releasing images of a second claimed multiple missile test[133] which took place three days after a first test?

Iran claimed nine missiles were tested. But US satellite tracking recorded only six. Why might that have been? The launch pictures and video were examined closely. Even amateurs quickly deduced the pictures released by the Revolutionary Guards through their media agency Sepah had been doctored. One of four apparent missile launches seen in images was a digital duplicate. Then a rocket launcher seen failing to fire in the video[134] had disappeared in the still photos. It was replaced by launching rocket with an identical smoke burn pattern to that of another rocket in the pictures. The Revolutionary Guards had used Adobe Photoshop or an equivalent to present an optimistic and far more upbeat image of missile capabilities than was probably the case.

'Let's add one more missile to spice up that picture, said the Mullahs' photoshop artists', was how the *Beirut Star*[135] sarcastically headlined the fakery as it showed the *New York Times* analysis of the doctored images.[136] 'A bit embarrassing considering the fact that the whole purpose of the picture is to show the west that "Iran is stronger than you think"' the newspaper concluded. One website cheekily went as far as to label the Iranian photographic devilry as 'fauxtography'.[137] In mocking mode it then showed how easily official images can be faked using cut-and-paste when there is no way to verify independently the originals. It even published an additional comic image of dozens of Iranian rockets apparently being fired in all directions during

[133] 10 July 2008.
[134] http://news.bbc.co.uk/1/hi/world/7501213.stm
[135] http://beirutspring.com/blog/2008/07/10/Iran-missile-pictures-were-fake/
[136] www.docstoc.com/docs/928916/Fake-Iranian-missile-photos
[137] http://littlegreenfootballs.com/article/30611_More_Iranian_Fauxtography_Discovered

another multiple test firing!

It has to be assumed that Iran launched several test missiles to convince world opinion of its ever growing ballistic capability eventually to launch nuclear weapons. But the faked images diluted the impact and achieved the opposite. They damaged any propaganda advantage the Iranian authorities hoped to gain for the status of their nuclear plans. In light of the exaggerated claims about test missile launches, what should be made of President Ahmadinajad's statement two weeks later that Iran did not just have 3,000 operational uranium enrichment centrifuges as stated in April, but 6,000?[138] Was that correct, or another exaggeration?

Iran's photographic own goal underlines the recurring question which remains unanswered. Why does there remain a reluctance by even the most developed and sophisticated institutions of power to embrace the implications for their credibility of how they handle such changing information dynamics in a crisis?

Israel: lessons learned in 2006 but not mastered in 2009

Israel's media experiences in 2006 and 2009 during their ferocious retaliation against Hezbollah in south Lebanon, then Hamas in Gaza, highlight vividly the institutional limits of dominating real-time information in a crisis.

In 2006, Israel's traditional assumptions of invincibility and military superiority were severely dented by a strategy and responses that proved inept.[139] The public impression of political and military failures was compounded by the official inability to control the media message on its terms. The information doer digital recording of much of what took place evaded military censorship. It was beamed live or in virtual real time by way of mobile phones and digital imagery, whether from the port city of Haifa, northern Galilee or southern Lebanon. The unprecedented level of information transparency meant that a rolling image of Israeli military ineffectiveness – and sometimes incompetence – was created almost instantly. After the impromptu military response to Hezbollah's seizing of three Israeli soldiers, Ehud Olmert's government found itself exposed by the way new media realities sidelined robust and long-established state procedures to control public perceptions. The Israeli government's power to limit public information in a security crisis involving national survival was lost, even though it was still guaranteed in theory by state censorship laws.

Unlike with the 2006 instant retaliation in south Lebanon, Israel had

[138] 'Nuclear Centrifuge Total has Doubled', *Observer* (27 July 2008), quoting the Associated Press.

[139] Detailed in full in the two reports of the investigating Public Commission chaired by Justice Dr Eliyahu Winograd, publ. Apr. 2007 and Jan. 2008.

the relative luxury in 2008 of having a year to plan in secret its operation against Hamas in Gaza. Officials confirm that central to this process was a detailed plan to control both the information flow and the media message. The belief in Jerusalem and Tel Aviv was that, with appropriate structures in place, at the official level they would be able to ride successfully the real-time information tiger. At the end of December 2008, Israel blocked all foreign media from entering Gaza and confined many to higher ground overlooking the Palestinians' narrow strip of land. The head of Israel's government press office, Danny Seaman, pre-emptively accused all foreign media of being 'unprofessional' and 'taking questionable reports at face value without checking'.[140]

Additionally, Israel's international projection of its case against Hamas became a relentless onslaught, using as many international media platforms as Israeli official voices could secure access to. In the first ten days of the 22-day operation these Israeli efforts to rectify the 2006 strategic deficiencies on real-time information largely worked. But an impressive media transparency inside Gaza had also taken shape. This meant that as its bombardment continued into its second week, Israel seemed to begin losing credible control of the media message. Video and eye witness evidence quickly emerged in Gaza of alleged targeting of unarmed civilians. This included a UN compound[141] and a house where IDF soldiers had herded families.[142] Israel's policy to 'shutdown' all independent media coverage did not prevent evidence emerging of what the UN's Relief and Works Agency alleged had been a 'war crime' against Palestinian refugees sheltering in a school.[143] This meant that by the end of its three-week operation Israel faced international calls for a war crimes trial because of alleged targeting of unarmed civilians.[144] 'The pictures do not lie', was the first line of a *Times* editorial which judged that 'Israel is better than its enemies' and its cause against Hamas was right. But the newspaper warned that 'the world expects better of it when children and civilians die under its ordnance. The past two weeks have damaged it [Israel] internationally . . .'[145]

Such accusations intensified further when emerging video and images seemed to confirm Israel's use of white phosphorous in ways that exceeded the use to screen troop movements that is allowed under the laws of war. The IDF initially denied its troops were firing white phosphorous shells at all. Then came growing 'information doer' and eye witness evidence of its

[140] 'Deal to Admit Journalists Aborted', *Guardian* (6 Jan. 2009).
[141] 7 Jan. 2009.
[142] 9 Jan. 2009.
[143] Incidents reported on 16 and 17 Jan. 2009.
[144] 'UN Chief Warns Israel over Gaza Family "Herded" into House that was Later Shelled: Attack Raises Threat of War Crimes Trial', *The Times* (10 Jan. 2009).
[145] 'In defence of Israel – No one can condone the civilian suffering in Gaza of the past two weeks. Nor should anyone doubt who is, in the end, responsible', *The Times* (10 Jan. 2009).

allegedly excessive use. The IDF confirmed an internal investigation had begun. Meanwhile Human Rights Watch filled the information space. After interviewing witnesses and detailed examination of ballistics fragments HRW concluded in a detailed 71-page report[146] that prima facie the IDF had 'deliberately or recklessly' fired white phosphorous at civilians in violation of the laws of war. This was 'evidence of war crimes' that 'must have required the approval of senior military officers'. At the time of HRW's publication the IDF had yet to publish any findings.

The official Israeli position that its Gaza operations only targeted Hamas fighters and fully respected the safety of civilians was then undermined further. The details published by the head of the Rabin pre-military preparatory course at Oranim Academic College from a remarkably frank debriefing on 13 February of junior IDF soldiers seemed to confirm the vivid impressions already created by 'information doer' material during the Gaza operation.[147] The IDF had issued permissive rules of engagement that meant commanders and their troops had no obligation to respect Palestinian civilians as unarmed non-combatants. They and their property could be targeted with lethal force if that was appropriate to serving Israel's war aims.

After its dreadful 2006 failure to secure control of the real-time information flow in south Lebanon and northern Galilee, Israel discovered once again the limits to official assumptions that the real-time media tiger can be both ridden and controlled successfully. Despite all the detailed planning to counter the new information transparency, Israel had largely failed. Too much digital data and imagery flowed from Gaza on multiple platforms in a host of ways that defied all Israel's control measures. None of what emerged helped the Israeli case to justify its operation to smash Hamas's military capability. Instead it undermined their claims, especially because of the way the IDF's official statements appeared to be tailored more for propaganda purposes than to make a realistic representation of what took place, including on apparent targeting errors. The BBC's Middle East Editor Jeremy Bowen wrote: 'far from controlling the news agenda, I think the Israelis have demonstrated that it can't be controlled in a world that is wired into a 24-hour news cycle'.[148]

But it is not as if the Israeli leadership did not appreciate the scale and implications of the new media dynamic at work. Six months after the 2006 war, Israel's then Foreign Minister and Deputy Prime Minister Tzipi Livni had revealed the price of such political vulnerability created by the new media

[146] Human Rights Watch, *Rain of Fire: Israel's Unlawful Use of White Phosphorous in Gaza* (New York: HRW, 25 Mar. 2009).

[147] First published by Danny Zamir, head of the course, in a newsletter. Then reported by Amos Harel, 'IDF in Gaza: Killing Civilians, Vandalism and Lax Rules of Engagement', *Ha'aretz* (19 March 2009). Also Donald Macintyre, 'Israel's Dirty Secrets in Gaza', *Independent* (20 March 2009)
James Hider, 'Israeli Soldiers Admit to Deliberate Killing of Gaza Civilians', *The Times* (20 March 2009)

[148] Jeremy Bowen, 'It Bothers Me that I Did Not Know their Names or their Story', *BBC Ariel* (20 Jan. 2009).

transparency in a crisis. She used a public frankness that was both alarming and refreshing.[149] She conceded that 'politicians no longer shape the agenda any more'. She added: 'The truth is that when it comes to international decision making, it is based on images and perceptions. Unfortunately sometimes, especially during the war in Lebanon, in which I asked my colleagues to support Israel . . . But I answered, look we have to give answers to the media. And we have to give answers to the public opinion. We cannot say what we believe in. But . . . there is something. The image of [the] Israel. And perceptions. And you have to deal with it.'

In 2009 Israel discovered again that, even with the most determined of efforts to overcome the new real-time information realities, there remain limits. And those limits are becoming more significant. Yet questioned in February 2009 Israeli diplomats dismissed such a negative analysis. They said that their government had been unfazed because in their long planning process they had always calculated those limits. They knew that much of the operation would be seen live on air and this would inevitably lead to global condemnation. The political calculation, however, was that what their government viewed as the vital military goal of destroying Hamas militarily must override any concerns about international outrage. In that, despite international condemnation, they believe they succeeded, despite only limited control of the real-time message.

Hurricane Katrina: how the media had better situational awareness than the US government

The experience of President George W. Bush during the Hurricane Katrina disaster along the Gulf Coast in 2005 was different. But eventually he had to be equally candid about how real-time media coverage had mercilessly exposed the political failings and vulnerabilities of his own executive power.

First, he had stayed on his Texas ranch while Katrina's unforgiving natural forces took hold. As the hurricane powered ashore, he was seen in Phoenix, Arizona, eating birthday cake and joking with Senator John McCain.[150] At the same time TV coverage and raw material from information doers and bloggers was confirming the overwhelming impact of storm waters inundating New Orleans. The deluge of coverage also revealed in detail the swift disintegration of everyday life, especially for the poor left behind. This included the evaporation of civilised norms and the questionable gun-law operations of the police and military. Only after two days was the President seen checking out the scale of this catastrophe in New Orleans for himself. But the White

[149] At the World Economic Forum, Davos, 26 Jan. 2007.

[150] 29 Aug. 2005.

House video showed him doing it briefly and cursorily from a porthole in his presidential aircraft flying at low level over the city en route from Texas to Washington, DC. This hardly allowed him to assess in person the appalling conditions, nor the rumours of gun crime and knifings, especially inside the impromptu refugee centre at the Superdome.

Politically, the impression left by the President's limited and belated concern was a catastrophe. The failings long remained seared on American memories and had a political, anti-Republican role in the outcome of the November 2008 election. Even worse was the apparent disconnect between public awareness of the dreadful scale of the hurricane disaster and the stark impression created of the inability of federal government agencies to cope. An administration re-elected in large part because of its promises to keep America safe in war and all forms of crisis had been seen to fail, and to fail very visibly.

Six months later Mr Bush volunteered a humiliating series of admissions. He conceded to a US TV interviewer that his federal government 'had not done as good a job as they should have done'.[151] He also made a frank confession of the weaknesses of federal and state governments when it came to handling real-time information. He revealed a core systemic weakness that, even in the heart of a major US city in crisis like New Orleans, there was 'no situational awareness'. This meant the federal authorities were 'not getting solid information awareness from people on the ground. And we need to do a better job.' He said one reason 'was because communications systems were wiped out'. Most significantly, the President then revealed that 'in many cases we were relying on the media who happened to have better situational awareness than the government! And when you have the media with better situational awareness than the government, the American people say "wait a minute! what is happening?"'

In so many ways Bush's frankness confirms the disconnect of time lines, the new vulnerabilities of policy-makers and the scale of public expectations created by the new information realities in every corner and political system in the world. This ubiquitous digital capacity is empowering the 'civilian surge' of *ad hoc* communities which increasingly challenge the status quo of traditional power and the official version of what is taking place. This is the case whether it occurs in the heart of one of the USA's most historic and iconic cities, or is being operated by the monks or separatist activists of Tibet,[152] the protesters in Burma, the rescue teams of an upturned liner off Antarctica,[153]

[151] *ABC World News Tonight*, 28 Feb. 2006.

[152] Tania Branigan, 'The Pilgrims Pray While Batons are Wielded and Tear Gas is Fired', *Observer* (16 Mar. 2008).

[153] 24 Nov. 2007.

or the anti-President protesters in the Philippines.[154]

In reflecting their acute personal discomfort at failings inside their governments during a major crisis, both Israeli Deputy Prime Minister Livni and President Bush were confirming candidly what others at their levels have reluctantly begun to concede in private. The new transparent realities of digital information mean power is shifting away from those given the elected responsibility to use it in a crisis. Livni confirmed in public what civil servants and commanders express in private: they face the increasingly unwinnable battle to counter real-time media 'images and perceptions'. And Bush admitted the scale of the public opinion hit for him and his administration's reputation when he confirmed how media reporting offers more 'awareness' of what is taking place in a crisis than a government has any chance of providing.

Hence the question posed throughout this study. Why in a major crisis does there continue to be this self-deluding mindset of denial for which ministers, civil servants, commanders and executives increasingly pay a very high price? Why do government and corporate power structures remain so slow, first to understand then to adapt fundamentally to this new information dynamic? But most critically – as highlighted by Israel's failed media policy during its 2009 Gaza operation – why do there remain assumptions that official might will always be right, and that the *ex-officio* power embedded in the institutions of state will always ensure information dominance?

The painful inability to embrace this reality into executive mindsets or bureaucratic processes with any noticeable momentum remains a major challenge, whatever the political or corporate system that is suddenly forced to confront it.

[154] On 20 Jan. 2001 the police and security services monitored 20 million text messages that organised the street protests of the Second People Power Revolution (which forced President Joseph Estrada from power over public disgust at alleged plunder and corruption).

8. Burma and China 2008: contradictory approaches to new realities

In states with governments elected by multi-party democracies the public can exercise ultimate sanction against any institution of political power that fails in a major crisis. Voters can always remove political leaderships from power. That 'civilian surge' of growing digital empowerment is forcing an enhanced level of accountability that a very senior former minister in a leading developed nation concedes is a 'real change to democracy'.[155]

Authoritarian governments face equal challenges to their credibility and reputation, but for different reasons. Encouragingly, at least one appeared suddenly to embrace the new realities during 2008, albeit perhaps only temporarily. But others did not. The contrast in approaches by different autocratic regimes is instructive for all governments. For them too, the impact of new media technologies has been shown to be as potentially 'subversive' as for highly developed democratic states. Yet policy responses have been diametrically different. In one case the doors to political transparency were flung open. In another they were slammed shut yet again.

Burma: street protests, a cyclone, and the 'skyful of lies'

The most profound negative example was the contemptuous attitude of Burma's governing junta to coverage of those escalating street protests in September 2007. The 'skyful of lies' described by the junta was a breathtaking flow of video and images filed by brave protesters via the ISPs of internet cafes in Rangoon, Mandalay and sometimes elsewhere. The *ad hoc* community of risk-taking information doers became empowered. Those undisputed and widely corroborated images swiftly challenged the authority and claims of the regime.

[155] Miliband, remarks, 4 Mar. 2008 (see n. 7).

In the first hours and days, a torrent of real-time images and reporting – both professional and amateur – confirmed instantly the scale of anti-government protests led by monks. The Burmese foreign minister's dismissive reference at the UN General Assembly to mere 'small protests hijacked by political opportunists'[156] seemed like nothing more than a politically correct phrase instinctively plucked from a propaganda manual of the past. Once again a default official response was to blame the Damn Meejah for exaggeration of an irrelevant aberration. Yet the digital images with their 'lies' had mobilised and outraged world opinion, especially at the UN Security Council. They achieved profound impact at a dramatic speed that the smuggled reports of the past and perhaps any images dribbling out a few days or weeks later would probably never have done.

Britain's Foreign Secretary, David Miliband, gripped the significance of the fundamental new dynamic in Burma, along with the new vulnerabilities for governments, whether fully democratic or authoritarian. At the height of the protests he highlighted how the video from Burma was confirming a 'much freer flow of information', which meant that for the institutions of power it is 'harder to hide'. He added: 'governments around the world need to know their actions will be seen'. Above all it is a 'very important part of the new diplomacy'.[157]

This analysis may seem obvious now. But at the time it was a radical break with the embedded political blindness to the new power of dramatic real-time media coverage to expose policy weaknesses in any unexpected crisis. Miliband's analysis could be readily dismissed as describing the obvious failings of an authoritarian regime freaked by its failure to control information in the way it normally does. But to slip willingly and submissively into that predictable groove of assumptions is to miss the confirmation of the impact on policy of the sweeping changes in technology. In times of acute tension, many in positions of power will still instinctively relate to the Burmese junta's contemptuous dismissal of a 'skyful of lies'. This includes figures in the most entrenched and stable of multi-party democracies. But it is self-delusion to default to such colourful Burmese-type descriptions which were more kneejerk propaganda than accurate analysis.

Burma in September 2007 highlights the extreme margins of the fundamental trend: the assumptions by those in power that they are right and have to be right; and that somehow the proliferation of information doer coverage is an outrageous misrepresentation or exaggeration, and therefore wrong. The fundamental reality in every system is that it is indeed 'harder to hide' and that there is a 'new diplomacy at work'. This has seismic political and

[156] 8 Oct. 2007.

[157] Doorstep remarks in London, 26 Sept. 2007.

corporate implications for all, whether the leaders of the Free World or those intolerant to the principles of multi-party democratic representation.

After the global impact of the protests revealed in September and October 2007, the Burmese leadership decided to confront the new reality and do all it could to eliminate any possibility that the 'Skyful of Lies' would be repeated. The security services relentlessly tracked down every ISP address, PC and individual used to transmit information and pictures. The human price paid was severe in both blood and personal freedoms.[158]

These autocratic instruments of oppression and shut down had been reinforced by the time Cyclone Nargis devastated vast areas of the Irrawaddy delta on 3 May 2008. For Nargis the challenge was not political, from dissent on the streets. It was humanitarian, from a massive natural disaster. Yet the overriding official instinct continued to be denial and shutdown. There was no independent corroboration of the scale of destruction and loss of life.[159] Foreign journalists and aid agencies were forbidden from entering the country. It had to be assumed that this was because of official fear of what they would see of the tens of thousands who had been killed, the 2.4 million displaced, and the inability of the regime to provide adequate aid.[160]

When the cyclone struck, it was quickly clear that the authorities would make sure that a repeat of the remarkable media transparency created by *ad hoc* information doers during the protests seven months earlier was firmly blocked. The sky would never again be filled with 'lies'! By and large they succeeded. But another element of the new generation of information-gathering realities still managed to outflank the Burmese government's determination to shut down access and independent scrutiny. A producer and camera operator from at least one major news organisation managed to enter the country on tourist visas. Before being arrested and deported they evaded security checks and military intelligence to record vivid video that confirmed the terrible impact and human cost of the cyclone. Hiding in ditches they beamed it out of the country on a new tiny, portable Bgan satellite uplink carried in a hiker's backpack. After several days operating covertly and transmitting ghastly images, the producer believed he had become 'the most wanted man in Burma'. Why, he later asked? His reporting was telling the world 'that the generals were lying, their aid operation was a farce, and people were going to die because of their wanton mismanagement'. Widely available commercial satellite imagery of the inundated delta further reinforced in

[158] 'Myanmar Blogger Jailed for 20 Years', *Straits Times* (12 Nov. 2008) reported the jailing of Nay Phone Latt, one of a dozen anti-government activists jailed that week.

[159] Peter Popham, 'Burma Raises Cyclone Death Toll to 78,000 But True Figures Much Higher', *Independent* (17 May 2008).

[160] The pooled external calculations of aid agencies up to three weeks after the cyclone. But the accuracy of these assessments remained unclear and under question for months.

global minds the scale of the disaster.

This time there was no Burmese government accusation of another 'skyful of lies'. But the official attitude was one of similar outrage. The emerging evidence from the handful of information doers able to record and transmit confirmed the obscenity of the Burmese claims that it had the resources and capability to cope.

Yet on real-time information the Burmese junta appeared to have neither learned nor changed. They did not modify their uncompromising policy between the political protests of September 2007 and the humanitarian disaster of May 2008. Their core instinct remained in place. During a major catastrophe they devoted significant security resources to tracking, shutting down and arresting anyone with the capacity to record and transmit details of the cyclone's impact. Yet on balance they only suceeded partially, not as sweepingly as they intended.

China: *weiji* – first a media crisis, than a media opportunity

During 2008 there was a fascinating and important comparison to be made between Burma and China over the handling of real-time information by an authoritarian government during similar, and almost simultaneous, political and humanitarian crises.

First, in March came the deeply uncomfortable political challenge to China's leadership from internal protests in Tibet. Much of it was confirmed vividly through video grabbed by eye witnesses or pro-independence activists using their mobile phones. The internet police and security services failed to block much of the material. In some cases, the footage was converted immediately to email files and uploaded via the internet. In other cases, digital SD cards were smuggled out by travellers. The angry reaction of the government and Communist Party to what emerged included deploying decisively the most conservative instincts of political control. 'The plots by the very few people against the stability and harmony of Tibet run counter to the will of the people and are doomed to fail', was the robust tone of official communiqués.[161] Beijing's response to media coverage of protests on the Greater Tibet plateau in March was a throwback to the traditional Party actions of clampdown, denial and propaganda during the Tiananmen Square protests in 1989.

Then two months later came the massive Sichuan earthquake. But this led to the sudden jettisoning of the same reactionary instincts of tight media control. Within two to three hours of the disaster unfolding, Chinese political

[161] Xinhua newsagency, 14 Mar. 2008.

instincts on information control apparently did a complete somersault. It can be argued that many institutions of power around the world could benefit from the positive lessons to be drawn from this new and uncharacteristic Chinese spirit of media enlightenment.

Some will caution that comparing the Chinese media handling of a major political challenge with the handling of a natural disaster is like comparing apples and pears, and is therefore invalid. But the Sichuan earthquake had potentially dark and swift political repercussions for the leadership in Beijing. During 2008 China showed how the media-handling instincts of institutions of power in one tightly controlled state can spin on the Chinese equivalent of a US dime and be of a very different order when required. There is no reason why all government systems wherever they are should not react in a similar way.

The political argument and debate at the highest level of China's government and Communist Party are unlikely ever to be revealed publicly. But the impact of Beijing's reversal in media policy during crises in a period of just eight weeks shows how embracing the new realities can produce very positive political results for public perceptions both of a government and of its leaders individually.

A base line for comparison is China's previous massive earthquake in Tangshan in July 1976. At that time, the government allowed only a belated three-line confirmation of the quake a few days later from the official China news agency. The true scale of the human toll and devastation only emerged three years later when officials confirmed quietly that more than 250,000 people had died.

In May 2008, a very different high-level political calculation was obviously made in Beijing within barely an hour of the quake. There was no way the scale of the Sichuan disaster could, or should, have been covered up. Despite what must have been instinctive objections and suspicions from the cadres of old-thinking Party conservatives, the key national leaders decided immediately they had to be seen very publicly to take charge and to be engaged in the catastrophe. This was even if the scale of the crisis was dire, and their personal presence would be more for show than practical, organisational advantage.

Later conversations with Chinese sources and foreign diplomats confirmed the impression at the time. Government and Party leaders realised immediately that their own political credibility was on the line because the majority of the Chinese population was now so digitally connected in the new information age. Resorting to traditional instincts of denial or a clampdown either to control or to limit the flow of detail was therefore not a viable option. Despite the intense political anger at what emerged during the unrest on the Greater Tibet Plateau in March, they had understood why a flow of images and information can no longer be shut down. Even with the overwhelming political imperative to ensure stability in advance of the Olympic Games in August, events in Tibet had confirmed a political price for not accepting the new realities of a transparent information environment.

So by the time of the Sichuan quake the Party, the government and its vast security structure had largely accepted they could not prevent the proliferation of information that would circulate instantly via the internet and the country's 620 million mobile phones.[162] They also knew that their image would be subject to instant public scrutiny. Any attempts at manipulation or deception would quickly be exposed by this new bottom–up information empowerment – the 'civilian surge'. There would be major negative consequences for the reputation of government leaders and the Party system if there was any suggestion of cover up of the scale of disaster. By contrast, there would be political gain from going 'open', with media coverage to match.

Instead of trying vainly to control the new real-time information reality in line with previous policy, there was a decision to harness it for political advantage.[163] After all, in Chinese the word for crisis *weiji* has two elements: *wei* means crisis and *ji* means opportunity. The Chinese leadership realised that the 'uncontrollable nature of mediated visibility' meant it was 'much more difficult to close the doors of the political arena and throw a veil of secrecy around it'.[164]

Within five hours Prime Minister Wen Jiabao had arrived in the earthquake disaster zone. His own confidence in the value of being seen to move so proactively had been established during ferocious winter storms three months earlier in February. With the road and rail transport systems seized up by heavy snow, he had chosen to visit railway stations, where he introduced himself by name to vast numbers of travellers stranded at the height of a national holiday. He could not guarantee to remove the snow. But he could raise their faith in his ability to issue the appropriate orders to the military and civilian authorities. Using a portable bull horn megaphone to make sure he was heard by the frustrated travellers (and recorded by a TV camera that accompanied him) he promised to make sure personally that the transport system would be unclogged. They would soon be moving again in time to enjoy the New Year with their distant families.

[162] This figure was confirmed in conversation with Wang Jianzhou, Chairman and Chief Executive of China Mobile, China's largest cellphone provider, on 26 Sept. 2008. The figure in Sept. 2007 was 501 million. Mr Wang also confirmed that this number is increasing by 6 million per month. The total figure will have risen considerably by the time you read this paper!

[163] Shi Anbin, professor of Media Studies at Tsinghua University, is quoted in *Newsweek International* (17 May 2008), 25, citing the three basic rules for communicating in a crisis: 'Tell the truth, tell it fast, and tell it first'. China neglected these principles during the Tibet crisis of Mar. 2008. 'Their earthquake response is the very first time they've lived up to international standards'.

[164] The author's requoting of principles identified in Thompson, 'New Visibility'.

As Prime Minister Wen flew from Beijing, full information transparency from the earthquake zone was already established. State controls on some blocked internet sites seemed to be lifted. Vivid video material recorded by Chinese amateur information doers on their mobile phones and digital cameras proliferated widely both inside China and beyond.[165] This meant that, unlike in previous major disasters such as that of 1976, the tragedy of Sichuan was instantly visible worldwide on YouTube, blog sites and all major international TV channels.

Within hours of the earthquake, on a proliferation of Chinese TV channels and internet platforms, Premier Wen was once again in the thick of a potential crisis of political credibility. He was seen kneeling amongst the quake rubble in a hard hat using a similar bull horn to shout reassurance to victims trapped under collapsed buildings. They should stay calm and patient. He would do his best to ensure that they and many thousands more were rescued. Wen was seen shouting 'every second lost could mean lives lost'.[166]

The favourable public reaction gave President Hu Jintao the confidence to follow his prime minister very publicly into the quake zone. The impact on public perceptions was equally positive. The remarkable decision of China's prime minister and then president first to fill, then dominate, the information space immediately after the quake, should be viewed as both inspired and wise. It carried political risk, but it paid off. There was never a political option to take the Burmese view and declare video and internet information emerging from Sichuan as just a 'skyful of lies'. Given the predominant official instincts of denial during moments of crisis, it was also a sharp lesson to others in high positions of power and responsibility around the world.

Overall, unlike the backlash over coverage of Tibet, this generated the kind of political dividend that the government and Communist Party needed in such a situation. A new, positive frontier seemed to have been crossed in how the institutions of government first understood, then embraced the need to join the race for information space in the first hours of a major crisis. In late June a smiling President Hu Jintao even made a point of being seen publicly in shirt sleeves at a PC terminal apparently having an 'online chat' and answering public concerns on the internet about the aftermath of the earthquake.[167] The jovial pictures sent a public message of an official willingness to engage. But the experience lasted only twenty minutes, which led to considerable scepticism. Did this gesture really mark a genuine lowering of the 'Great Digital Firewall'

[165] Jamil Anderlini and Geoff Dyer, 'Amid the Mud, Fireworks Signal Another Body', *Financial Times* (14 May 2008).

[166] Mary Hennock and Melinda Liu, 'The Sichuan Earthquake Could Change the Way Chinese See their Leaders', *Newsweek* (26 May 2008).

[167] Jeremy Page, 'Hu Pokes his Head over "Great Firewall" to Seek the Opinions of 221m Netizens', *The Times* (24 June 2008), 29.

and a fundamental shift in official acceptance of the 'civilian surge' of public empowerment on information? Or was it just a propaganda distraction and a timely reassertion of official power? Overall, had it just been the latest in a lengthening line of 'regular spasms of control and loosening up'?[168]

Later arrests of some distraught parents of quake victims, who used the internet to campaign to discover why school buildings collapsed, suggested that any new media enlightenment might be one of those short-lived spasms. So did the official orders to the Chinese media not to report the allegations of poor school design and construction standards, along with the burgeoning complaints of corruption.[169] In many ways this was a swift return to type.

It must therefore be asked: given the contrasts between the Chinese handling of the Tibet protests and the Sichuan earthquake, is the new official enlightenment on information handling in a crisis irreversible, or will there always be a return to traditional instincts?

In the post-earthquake period after May, the Chinese media reported crises of all kinds largely openly. But it was still under official direction that on occasions initially censored details or delayed publication. During the weeks leading up to the Olympics in August 2008 there continued to be signs of institutional uncertainty, discomfort and an instinctive return to the traditional comfort zones. There were plenty of foreign media complaints of 'wanton violation' of press freedoms,[170] the 'push-back' on accreditation or reporting requests,[171] and the blocking of overseas websites.[172] This was despite the official commitment to 'complete freedom' to report on all aspects of China.[173]

On the one hand there were dark examples of control. BBC reporter John Sweeney tried 'holding them to their promise' when before the Olympics he tried to report on the post-earthquake situation and local corruption with 'no permit to be there'. Sweeney concluded: 'every time I try to talk to someone they are scared off. The story is being closed down.'[174] The overriding imperative remained 'maintaining overall social and political stability'. Isabel Hilton, editor of Chinadialogue.net, believed that 'old instincts have reasserted themselves'.[175] On the other hand there was fragmentary evidence of enlightened attitudes. The leading US China analyst, Professor Kenneth Lieberthal, told the US Congress in July 2008: 'I was in China directly after

[168] See Mark Leonard, *What does China Think?* (London: Harper Collins, 2008), 17.
[169] Tom Mitchell, 'Beijing Reins in Quake Coverage', *Financial Times* (1 June 2008).
[170] Mure Dickie and Justine Lau, 'Attack on Journalists Puts China under Fire', *Financial Times* (26/27 July 2008).
[171] James Doran, 'Beijing Lays Down the Law for Army of Global Media', *Observer* (27 July 2008).
[172] Mure Dickie, 'Beijing's Block on Websites to Hit Journalists', *Financial Times* (31 July 2008).
[173] See articles cited in nn. 164–5 above.
[174] BBC *Panorama*, 4 Aug. 2008.
[175] During discussion on the BBC's *Dateline London* on 2 Aug. 2008.

the earthquake, and it was obvious that something new is going on, with the Communist Party explicitly [even] thanking NGOs for their effective assistance.'[176]

How China's leaders chose to embrace these new and often extreme manifestations of the fast-growing, but irreversible information transparency in a crisis will remain uncertain. But on balance, despite some clear reversals, they seem to be sending public signals of a determination to come to terms with them more positively. In a series of candid replies during an interview on 28 September 2008, Prime Minister Wen Jiabao told CNN[177] that 'I frequently browse the internet'. This confirmed that he had joined almost 300 million Chinese who do the same,[178] with access to 'a lot of postings that are quite critical of the government'. In saying this Mr Wen seemed to suggest a growing sense of political approval – or at least acceptance – for the role of the internet in Chinese life, even if limits 'to uphold state security' remain. He even volunteered the need for what he called a new 'oversight by the news media and other parties' of government activity. Open complaint and criticism must be embraced. Again, such words seemed to fit a new conceptual political framework emerging after what Mr Wen described as months of 'grave challenges to the Chinese government and people'. He accepted that negative public perceptions of the government's handling of the crises over snow, the pre-Olympic Tibet protests, the Sichuan earthquake and the contaminated baby milk scandal had tested the leadership's credibility. The dramatic impact in China of the world economic crisis in late 2008 compounded even more harshly the scale of the political real-time challenge.

In his CNN interview Mr Wen also spoke openly about the massive challenge of how to maintain public confidence during crises with the new levels of information transparency. At the same time as China began to face 'considerable difficulties' from the global financial meltdown, he used a prepared speech[179] to clarify new principles as to how to mitigate the impact of a major emergency on public confidence. 'We will create conditions that allow people to criticise and supervise the work of the government more effectively, and foster a lively political environment.' He added: 'We will further deepen and broaden opening up. Opening up also means reform.' Then in subsequent spontaneous questioning about his own immediate public engagement in the snow and earthquake crises Mr Wen said that leaders like him 'should not fear difficulties with disasters'. They 'should have the courage to rise to challenges

[176] Testimony to House Foreign Relations Committee, 23 July 2008.

[177] Interview with Fareed Zakaria of *Newsweek* on CNN, broadcast 28 Sept. 2008. See www.asiafinest.com/forum/lofiversion/index.php/t175178.html

[178] 298 million internet users confirmed by the China Internet Network Centre on 13 Jan. 2009. The increase was 42% year on year. At the same time the US had 233 million internet users.

[179] Speech to the World Economic Forum meeting in Tianjin, China, on 27 Sept. 2008

and not be daunted by them', and they must respond with 'resolute measures'.

Late in 2008, with internet and mobile phone figures rising inexorably, came an official commitment to keep in place the principle of 'complete freedom'. This was even though the reality during the pre-Olympic period had fallen far short of the openness apparently promised. Based on the political culture and past performance, big suspicions remained about true official intentions. Yet again, it could all have been words to counter fast-growing resentments and to buy time. There is, after all, a long history of leadership fears and 'stunts' to exploit media power.[180]

And after December 2008, the contradictory signals continued. The overseas Chinese websites of several western media organisations were again blocked for a time, and then unblocked. A Belgian TV crew complained to the Foreign Ministry that they were pulled from their vehicle, beaten and had their notes taken while reporting on AIDS sufferers in Henan.[181] By the end of 2008, Chinese diplomatic sources were going out of their way to give the impression that in Beijing 'significant lessons' had been learned at high levels about 'mistakes that were made' during the media handling of the year's crises. Accepting 'greater openness' had to be the new reality, however steep any political costs might turn out to be.

But the obvious internal tensions remained, even if the official signals were more disguised. Continuing limits became apparent in late March 2009 when YouTube confirmed the slowing and blocking of its video stream in China on 23 March.[182] This appeared to be an official reaction to the posting on 20 March by the Tibet government-in-exile of new unauthenticated mobile phone video. It showed the apparent vicious beating of monks and civilians during protests in Tibet one year earlier on 14 March 2008. There was no official Chinese confirmation that the posting of this video had led to the blocking of YouTube. But there were grounds for suspicions.[183] The official newsagency Xinhua quoted an unnamed official in Tibet who said that the three video excerpts showed the 'Dalai Lama group' were 'fabricating lies'. He added: 'technology experts found that video and audio was edited to piece together different places, times and people'. There was no consensus among the sometimes heated postings on blog sites as to whether the videos were authentic or elaborate official fakes designed to discredit the Dalai Lama on the politically sensitive 50th anniversary of the failed uprising against Chinese rule in Tibet.

[180] Leonard, *What does China Think?*

[181] 'China Looks into Attack on Belgian Journalists': report by the AP in *International Herald Tribune* (3 Dec. 2008).

[182] Tania Branigan, 'China Blocks You Tube'. *Guardian* (25 March 2009) http://www.guardian.co.uk/world/2009/mar/25/china-blocks-youtube

[183] Jane Macartney. 'Great Firewall of China blocks access to YouTube, again'. *Times* (25 March 2009) http://www.timesonline.co.uk/tol/news/world/asia/article5972245.ece

Yet overall, such moments of political equivocation or uncertainty could not reverse the profound impact of a sharp information empowerment in China that had been enabled by the explosive growth in digital technology over the previous three years. In public at least, the official message continued to be one of a new political pragmatism. By 27 March YouTube was functioning normally again inside China. At the height of the YouTube concerns a foreign ministry spokesman had made a point of saying: 'Many people have a false impression that the Chinese government fears the internet. In fact, it is just the opposite.'[184]

However, the evidence often remained contradictory. On the one hand, there were tragic examples of the human cost of using the new technology to shed light in what traditionally have been dark corners of Chinese life. Old authoritarian instincts still encouraged many officials to shut down brutally the new community accountability in China that was being encouraged both by the leadership in Beijing and the exponential acquisition rate of mobile phones. The challenge from information doers was the new power to defy and reveal, even at what was sometimes a considerable personal price.[185]

On the other hand video footage taken on mobile phones frequently succeeded in exposing official brutality and abuses of power, and in turn changed policy. One video shot by an 'information doer' peasant farmer showing outrageous acts of violence by thugs acting for a regional government and a power company during a land grab[186] became emblematic of the trend. It confirmed publicly the reality of the 87,000 protests and other 'incidents of discontent' reported by the internal security organs in 2005.[187] Officials confirm that this new level of community transparency was a pivotal driver that forced modifications of policy in the National People's Congress and Party Congress to create a 'new socialist countryside'.[188]

Any very public highlighting of political failings via the new level of information transparency makes the leadership in Beijing nervous because of its potential to fuel a public and social backlash against them. As Professor Lieberthal described this political dilemma to the US Congress: 'The Communist Party [in China] is both supportive of greater popular involvement in managing affairs and uneasy about where this might lead.'[189] This growing political challenge became much sharper in late 2008 and early 2009. With

[184] Remarks by Foreign Ministry spokesperson Qin Gang on 24 March 2009.

[185] On 10 Jan. 2008 the *People's Daily* reported that 24 residents of Tianmen, a city in Central China's Hubei province, were detained after Wei Wenhua, the general manager of a company owned by the local water resources bureau, was pulled out of his car and savagely beaten for videoing the clash between villagers and officials.

[186] See the video shot by a peasant farmer of a violent land grab by a power company on 11 June 2005.

[187] These were the latest figures published officially.

[188] See statements of the final outcome of the 2006 National Peoples' Congress. http://news.bbc.co.uk/1/hi/world/asia-pacific/4775350.stm

[189] Lieberthal, 23 July 2008 (see n. 170).

export markets contracting, factories closing and vast numbers of workers being made redundant at a rate that far exceeded official predictions,[190] the country's economic implosion began to threaten the stability of the state and the Communist Party's control. The social cost and impact was covered extensively in community internet sites. This meant state media outlets had no option but to carry coverage or they would risk the inevitable accusation of censorship or news management. Even the state news agency Xinhua started to raise publicly the spectre of mass protests over job losses and contracting economic opportunities.[191]

As the economic tsunami hit China,[192] this information dynamic forced unprecedented public questions on the issue of social stability to Prime Minister Wen Jiabao. The nature of both his prepared remarks and subsequent spontaneous answers in front of large global audiences seemed to further confirm that a fundamental adjustment to the new realities of information transparency was underway. Mr Wen signalled an important political recalculation designed to come to terms with new media pressures in a crisis. In its own small way this was confirmed in February 2009 when a protester threw a shoe at the prime minister during a high-profile appearance at Cambridge University in the UK. Traditionally there was no way such an open challenge to a Chinese leader – if it ever took place – would have been aired on Chinese Central TV, CCTV. But on this occasion it had to be shown, albeit belatedly.[193] This was because video of the attack was already circulating widely on internet sites in China. It meant many Chinese already knew about the incident and had seen it for themselves. As a result, officials must have concluded it would be odd for the video not to be seen on CCTV's coverage of an official prime ministerial visit.

Unlike Burma's junta, China's leadership learned in 2008 the need to build new working principles to embrace the impact of media openness and real-time information on their political decision-making. The Skyful of Lies was in reality a new Skyful of Truths that can rarely be denied or suppressed.

The new common vulnerability for top–down information handling

After their different experiences managing acute crises, Chinese Prime

[190] On 2 Feb. 2009 the Xinhua newsagency reported that the number of jobless Chinese migrants had doubled from 10m in Dec. 2008 to 20m: www.nytimes.com/2009/02/03/world/asia/03china.html
[191] Forecast carried in *Outlook Weekly* (Xinhua, 6 Jan. 2009).
[192] Phrase taken from the warning by Victor Chu, Chairman First Eastern Investment Group, in the BBC World Debate recorded in Tianjin on 28 Sept. 2008.
[193] 'Shoe Hurled at Chinese PM: Unusually State TV Broadcasts Footage of the Embarrassing Incident', *Times of India* quoting agencies (4 Feb. 2009).

Minister Wen Jiabao and US President George W. Bush seem belatedly to have drawn the same conclusions about the limits of their *ex-officio* power. So, too, had former Russian president Vladimir Putin eight years earlier. In the hours and days after the submarine *Kursk* K-141 sank during a live firing exercise in the Barents Sea on 12 August 2000, Putin remained out of public view on holiday in his Black Sea dacha. During that period, the information space was overwhelmed by rumours unfavourable to the Russian navy. Admiral Popov, commander of the Arctic fleet, lied to journalists based on his aircraft carrier about the *Kursk*'s fate. He protested to them that nothing was amiss, even though he already knew that an explosion on the submarine had sunk the vessel. Putin left the same impression: he remained aloof and continued the appearance of vacation-as-usual, even as first confirmations emerged via Russian websites and naval chatter that the *Kursk* was lost. In 2008, Putin – as Prime Minister – had very different instincts. On 11 August, the fourth day of the South Ossetia crisis, he made a point of flying directly from the Olympic opening ceremony in Beijing to be seen by TV cameras engaged with Russian troops in North Ossetia during the Russian military intervention into Georgia.

Even in an authoritarian or near authoritarian state, the new media realities of transparency, with the likelihood of information doers proliferating, mean leaders must assume there is no escape from public oversight and scrutiny. To fail to embrace these new realities and prepare for them can now carry the highest political price, whether in a dirigiste one-party nation or a liberal, multi-party democracy.

9. The perspective: present and future?

It is hard to recall the basic reality just a few years ago. Connectivity was reliant on hard wires, basic analogue technology and the ability to pay for a relatively exclusive telecom experience. Media recording and reporting, plus the profession of journalism, were relatively exclusive preserves. Now, without question, low-cost, digital recording and transmission technology are uniformly taken for granted. This is not just in the developed world but across fast growing tracts of the developing world.

The implications of this new level of empowerment are profound but still, in many ways, unquantifiable. However, central to this dynamic are the rapidly developing societal implications, especially the relationship between a fast-changing media environment and institutional power. As a result, there has to be a new definition of the media. It should no longer be the relatively narrow, exclusive preserve that is traditionally assumed. It must be a vastly broader, almost infinite, digital landscape. Here the casual motivated spectator with a digi-phone can often have a more significant role than the traditional, professional media bearer of witness who either is dispatched to the crisis zone or might happen to be present.

The technology and the resulting transparency created by it have starkly overturned many of the established assumptions of power and information flows. They allow the instant bearing of witness by almost anyone with the modest amount of cash now needed to buy a mobile phone with a camera lens, or just a plain standard digital camera.

Political, military or corporate leaders must acknowledge urgently the scale of change and the need to recalibrate their understanding of the media environment that now both challenges and threatens them. If they do not, their institutional vulnerability will increase, with even more dire and irreversible implications for their reputations and image.

In the introduction to this discussion paper I wrote that the trends of the dynamic relationship between a dramatically changing media environment and policy-making have been relentless. In many ways they have been predictable. But because of the institutional denial the responses have not been.

That institutional denial remains largely in place. It has not substantively been moved by new real-time information dynamics, however sharp and painful. That is why the most obvious remains the most elusive. If any lessons are learned they still often seem to be lessons then ignored or forgotten. Any proactive responses tend not to be by way of pre-emption. The best tends to be hastily reworking experiences of the last crisis, but far too late.

This author remains reluctant to offer prescriptions to government, non-government and corporate bodies whose images and reputations have been rendered more brittle and vulnerable. No journalist should offer advice to those he has to report on and – in my case – challenge with difficult questions. I – and hopefully my colleagues – would not, or at least should not, take much notice of a minister, civil servant or corporate executive who tries to tell us how a media organisation should run its news operation! So in similar vein, why should a government or corporation that is concerned ultimately about its accountability to either the public or its shareholders take notice of a journalist's recommendations on improving their information handling capacity and policy in moments of tension or crisis?

However, such has been the impact of my findings that there is pressure for me to go beyond just analysing the dynamic. 'So what do we (or they) do?' is the frequent coda of questions after presentations. To the obvious frustration of participants, that firewall of journalistic responsibility is the explanation – or some will say excuse – for declining to offer advice. Until now, that self-denying ordinance has held. But now, because of the nature of the findings in this study, there is an obligation to go further and offer recommendations. This I have done willingly.

Recommendations

The single most critical recommendation is as simple as the challenge is obvious: throw open the institutional windows, pull down those mind-walls and shed those feet of clay. Then there will be understanding of the process and nature of the real-time dynamic that so profoundly undermines official assumptions of information superiority.

If the mind-walls remain up, and the mindsets stay embedded in the institutional equivalent of concrete, then any capacity to respond will remain leaden, belated and inadequate. But if these embodiments of denial are broken up and dismantled then there can be progress from that 'different age' of past thinking to the embracing of current realities. No longer will the 'information doers', 'born digitals' or 'motivated amateurs' be viewed as odd, marginal or alien forces that are inconvenient, threatening and come from a shadowy, incomprehensible alternative planet. Instead these new forces of information empowerment will be viewed as inevitable irritants whose new power is well understood and can be handled effectively.

Therefore:

- Embrace the fundamental new media dynamics of transparency identified in this discussion paper. The imperative is to enter the information space swiftly and report whatever is clear and known, however little that is.
- Accept the infinitely broader and deeper definitions of the media matrix. The new landscape goes well beyond the traditional, narrow institutional assumptions of what constitutes the media. There is a pivotal role for the new generation of 'information doers'. It must be assumed they are everywhere with an inherent capability to produce a 'civilian surge' of real-time information. Engage them; embrace their new role; do not resist them.
- Assume it is 'harder to hide' and that there is little chance of escape from public oversight and scrutiny. Accept that the professional price for ignorance and naïveté about media will often be witheringly high.
- Accept that while working to control the information high ground must be a central requirement of policy delivery, dominating it is increasingly unlikely in a crisis. If that turns out to be the case then accept it as a reality, not a policy failure.
- Don't view the new real-time information realities as a threat but an opportunity. Identify those elements of the fast-growing, almost infinite multi-media language where you can compete effectively for the information high ground, then do so with self-confidence.
- In public, create the impression and reality of a new level of assertive engagement on real-time information in a crisis, however vulnerable the reality may feel behind the scenes. Do not continue the culture of being backward about coming forward.

- Debate internally the dilemmas of *F3*: whether to act *first* and *fast*, and if so how to handle the risk of being *flawed* in doing so. Accept there can be a perilously fine line between successful and disastrous interventions. But also accept that *not* to enter the immediate post-crisis media space will often carry a higher cost than entering it imperfectly. The aim must remain to act assertively and swiftly in the hope of commanding that space, however briefly or incompletely.
- Work on the assumption that handling real-time information will at best be a zero sum game. If more is achieved, then you have been lucky and done well. There will be occasions when the nature of government, or institutional or corporate power in any civil system, will produce the expected information control. But it should never be assumed, or taken as given. Indeed, it is more realistic to assume the opposite.
- Remove any entrenched institutional resistance to being forced to feed the news beast. From top to bottom retrain or remove the 'courtiers' who 'ratchet up old means of control' and 'like behaviour that masks the truth'. Actively promote both a comfortable understanding of the new dynamic and a psychological retooling as forces for enhancing careers, not destroying them.
- Develop new, internal, quick-response information flows for the multi-platform environment that are smart and rapid. They must cut through established top–down, hierarchical structures that often hold up the kind of rapid internal traffic of priority information needed in a crisis.
- Institutionally, leave no impression that a hasty mis-speak or misrepresentation in public will lead to internal criticism, a dressing down or even blocking of a career. In authoritarian top–down structures, any deviation from a robustly ordained policy line or culture is often feared as a career killer. The reality must be the opposite. Ensure it is understood that empowerment and devolution of responsibility are a career enhancer that carries no professional risk, even if mistakes are made.
- Exploit the instinctive grasp of these new real-time dynamics among the next generations in your organisation. Have faith in that grasp, even if they hold more junior positions and have no executive authority. Even if they have little to say

in the first stages of a crisis, it should be hoped that through their self-confident performance in public they will ease fears and suspicions by filling the post-crisis media space.

- Shed the instincts of hierarchy and the need for executive control from the highest level. Have professional confidence in those employed at all levels. Empower the more junior officers, NCOs, officials, executives and public servants to respond. They must be encouraged to search rapidly for basic relevant data relating to a crisis, and then have the confidence to use it in a timely way to join the crowded post-crisis information space.
- Devolve responsibility for handling real-time information to lower levels of 'mission command'. They should be well trained and granted enhanced levels of empowerment. This will allow far more timely responses that match the 'tyranny of the time line' and compete on comparable terms in the 'race for space'.
- There is always a risk that public post-crisis announcements might deviate from those preferred by the most senior officials or executives at the top or centre. But such possible disadvantage are significantly outweighed by the likelihood of a decisive and self-confident entrance into the information space. Some form of appearance is far better than silence and nothing being said.
- If possible create a ready checklist (on a plasticised card) to give to staff as guidance for the basic facts to be sought first in a crisis.

Next stages for analysis

As made clear in the introduction to this study, tying down the trends has been like shooting at a constantly moving target. By the day and by the hour the information dynamic dives and soars, at times almost defying all efforts to capture the essence. This has been the most up-to-date snapshot possible of a never-ending process. The text and conclusions are not definitive. They have offered new vantage points and springboards for further analysis and insight. The aim of a discussion paper is to promote just that – discussion. The hope is to encourage not only a spirit of both confirmation and clarification, but also challenges and disagreements. It is hoped they will be forthcoming from corporate executives, politicians, civil servants, military officers and colleagues across the media. That should be the next stage of this study.

Acknowledgements

More than ever, the process of producing news involves a Rubik's cube of media colleagues and players, most of whom work for other organisations, themselves or no one in particular. As a presenter I rarely meet or even get to know them personally. Each is part of the complex global grid of editorial input and responsibilities that somehow fuses together remarkably through a major multi-platform news organisation like the BBC. They make vital contributions to creating on-air output which has journalistic shape, logic and impact.

The work of so many unknown and unnamed 'colleagues' who contribute to this grid is central to the new media dynamic that I highlight in this study. In the field, TV cameramen and women have always used great risk, boldness and cunning to record the images that vividly bring alive global developments. They and the traditional breed of reporters have now been joined by what this study identifies as the *ad hoc* generation of 'information doers' who are the new electronic eyes and ears of the news media business. I salute their work and thank them all for their initiative and often their bravery.

My enormous appreciation also goes to the large numbers of BBC News colleagues who hourly on the continuous news channels like BBC World News create editorial form and sense from the increasingly overwhelming multitude of editorial inputs. In so many ways, their working dilemmas at all levels – which we often experience together – are at the heart of this paper. Without their off-screen skills and tenacity, an on-screen presenter like myself would often be as helpless as a beached whale.

The proposal for this paper came during a conversation with John Lloyd on a bus during a rainstorm in northern Italy. As the final elements of the new Reuters Institute for the Study of Journalism were coming together in Oxford, the project would capture the essence of one of its core ambitions: to analyse the role and impact of fast-changing media realities on decision-making and public perception. As Director of Journalism, John's robust capacity to convene and advise on editorial issues took forward the principle. He provided a vital beacon that both energised new approaches and focused editorial outcomes, all of which were invaluable and much appreciated.

I am deeply grateful to Hew Strachan, Chichele Professor of the History of War at Oxford University, for the detailed reviewing of my drafts and the vital expert guidance offered at many key stages, in particular because of the new reputational issues raised for the military and civil servants. I am also most grateful for comments and further insights in the final stages from Professor Sir Lawrence Freedman, and former ambassadors Sir Jeremy Greenstock and Jeremy Kinsman. Andrew Roy, Head of News at BBC World News, was – as usual – more generous with his time than the hourly news pressures should have allowed. I much appreciated his commitment to reading the text and offering me wise counsel on some points.

I extend enormous appreciation to David Levy, the institute's new director. He took office at a late and critical stage in the preparation of the discussion paper. While absorbing all the challenges of the new job, he engaged in a masterful way in the business of overseeing the editorial process to ensure the timely publication intended during that original rainstorm. David's guidance was supplemented by valuable additional thoughts from Glenda Cooper, Visiting Fellow at the RISJ, because of her own work in fields related to issues in this paper.

My immense thanks also go to a large number of ministers, former ministers, civil servants, corporate executives, academics and others somehow involved in disciplines impacted by the information dynamics of the new media realities. A small number attended brainstormings in which my ideas were tested and modified. Others discreetly helped out with their thoughts and observations. Many willingly supported and engaged in what I was researching, but wanted no formal identification or recognition that might be traceable. Others helped me in a variety of ways, often without knowing fully the reasons behind our discussion or my questions.

Finally, the warmest of appreciation and affection is due to my wife Judy. Yet again she somehow put up with my absences, either on assignments related to the focus of this paper, or while I worked in my study late at night and early in the morning to assemble and fine-tune my thoughts as the target issues kept evolving. All of this while I kept the on-air day job going presenting for BBC World News in Studio N8 at BBC TV Centre.

This paper is written in a personal capacity and does not reflect BBC policy or views. Any errors are mine alone.

London, 27 April 2009